ON WOLVES AND FINANCE

ON WOLVES AND FINANCE

The Connection between Business, Biology, and Physics

Zach De Gregorio

ESBEE BOOKS

This book contains information on investing. Investing is risky, and it is possible to lose all or, in some cases, more than your initial investment. It is recommended to contact a professional advisor before making investments. Neither the publisher nor author shall be liable for any loss of profit or any other commercial damages, including but not limited to special, incidental, consequential, or other damages.

ISBN-13: 978-0-6922-5483-7

ESBEE BOOKS
Albuquerque, NM
www.esbeebooks.com
For inquiries contact info@esbeebooks.com
Printed in the United States of America

To the dreamers

To those who think outside the box

To the artists and scientists, who may be one and the same

To the business men and women who have a passion for creating value

To those who believe that together we can accomplish great things

This book is for you

TABLE OF CONTENTS

INTRODUCTION

In 2013, a surprising announcement highlighted a growing conflict within the business community: both Eugene F. Fama and Robert J. Shiller received the Nobel Prize in economics. The decision was ironic because Fama and Shiller often have conflicting views on the very nature of economics. Fama is from the University of Chicago's School of Business, which is known for supporting the Efficient-Market Hypothesis. Under this theory, economic models are based on individuals making rational choices. In contrast, Shiller is from Yale University's School of Business, which is known for behavioral finance. Shiller argues that consumers often make irrational purchases, and behavioral decisions drive markets rather than mathematical calculations.[1]

These two conflicting views present compelling arguments about how markets work. Research shows that rational economic models do represent market movements in a general sense. However, someone only needs to witness erratic drivers on any American freeway to realize that people around them often make irrational decisions.

The conflicting views of Fama and Shiller essentially reflect the struggle of many business men and women with the gap between economic theory and every day experience. Theory is meant to provide an abstraction that can assist in making better decisions in real-life situations. It is only natural for someone to question why so many experiences have different outcomes than economic models would suggest.

In the case of Fama and Shiller, the gap is significant. There remain many unexplained business scenarios where the stakes are high. For instance, "market panics" have no place in perfect economic models where supply always meets demand. On the other hand, if the economic models are not effective, how can one make an informed decision during a market panic? It is difficult to make decisions when there is such glaring discrepancies around how markets work.

Ultimately, neither Fama nor Shiller succeed in closing the gap between theory and experience. Unfortunately, this gap of knowledge contains some of the most fundamental questions in business.

- Why do societies have rich and poor?
- Why do economies grow the way they do?
- Why do we continue to have a business cycle of boom and bust?

After decades of research, we still do not understand some of the fundamental issues in business. It is not that Fama or Shiller are wrong. On the contrary, the research of both these men truly changed the world. But I suspect there is a new element that is not yet captured in current economic thought. These questions require a new theoretical model that explains both perspectives of peaceful markets where supply meets demand, as well as markets that do not always allocate resources effectively. Such a theory would explain the phenomenon of vast income inequality, explosive growth, and cycles of boom and bust.

With such opposing views on economics, many consider these questions unanswerable. They assume that markets and people are either random or too complex to be explained through theory. I would like to suggest an alternative approach. I believe it is worth seeking a theoretical framework that explains the fundamental questions in business and closes the gap between theory and experience. If there are not explanations in the academic literature, it means we have not found all the answers yet.

Eight Fundamental Finance Equations

Dividend Pricing Model

$$P = \frac{D}{r - g}$$

Capital Asset Pricing Model (CAPM)

$$r_i = r_f + \beta(r_m - r_f)$$

Arbitrage Pricing Theory (APT)

$$r_j = r_f + b_{j1}RP_1 + b_{j2}RP_2 + \cdots + b_{jn}RP_n$$

Weighted Average Cost of Capital (WACC)

$$WACC = \frac{E}{D+E} * r_e + \frac{D}{D+E} * r_d * (1-t)$$

Modern Portfolio Theory (MPT)

$$E(R_p) = \sum_i w_i \, E(R_i)$$

Black-Scholes Formula

$$C(S,t) = N(d_1)S - N(d_2)Ke^{-r(T-t)}$$

$$d_1 = \frac{\ln\left(\frac{S}{K}\right) + (r + \frac{\sigma^2}{2})(T-t)}{\sigma\sqrt{T-t}}$$

$$d_2 = d_1 - \sigma\sqrt{T-t}$$

Economic Value Added (EVA)

$$EVA = (ROIC - WACC) * K = NOPAT - WACC * K$$

Jensen's measure (alpha)

$$a_p = r_p - \left[r_f + \beta_p(r_m - r_f)\right]$$

Figure 1. Eight fundamental finance equations.

The study of finance contains several other examples of academic uncertainty. Scholars created financial equations, based on economic theory, as a means to perform valuations. Since there are certain market situations that economic theory does not explain, these equations will also return nonsense answers under certain conditions. Uncertainty in financial issues is understandable, because the field is still a young discipline. Major investment in business research only really began in the 1950s.

I do not suggest that decades of research are wrong, but it is reasonable to assume that our understanding of business is incomplete. Everything in finance derives from about eight fundamental equations (**Figure 1**).[2] These equations can be used in combination to make decisions on how to manage a financial portfolio. Finance today is much more complex, but still builds upon the concepts from these basic equations. These equations are valuable in that they provide important insights into the nature of business. However, if you were to build a computer simulation of an economy, based only on these equations, it would be difficult to recreate the market dynamics we experience. Disconnects remain between financial theory and our experience in markets.

I propose there is a missing equation. It is possible that a new equation could close the gap between theory and experience. This new approach creates a framework that explains previous financial equations in a more realistic context. I refer to this new equation as the **Theory**

of Credit Markets. This book is an abstract of my research in theoretical finance over the last seven years. Part I defines the key elements of credit markets. Part II explores some of the defining features of growth. Part III crystalizes these concepts into the Theory of Credit Markets. Part IV provides examples of practical applications in every day finance. And Part V identifies the larger implications of this theory for business, biology, and physics.

Part I : THE THEORY OF INEQUALITY

Transactions as debt arrangements

Economic Models are often incomplete. They look at each transaction from one person's perspective. The flaw in this approach is there are always at least two people involved in each transaction. In overlooking the impact of multiple parties, economic models miss an important element of market dynamics. I propose that a new framework, called the **Theory of Inequality**, overcomes these weaknesses. I will show how this new approach to understanding transactions provides valuable insight for business decisions.

To switch economic models from one perspective to two, it is necessary to rethink all transactions as debt arrangements. Economics tends to frame everything as a cash transaction from one person's perspective. Consider the major finance equations (**Figure 1.** Eight fundamental finance equations.). These equations describe one person evaluating an economic situation and arriving at the best solution. Instead of one perspective, a debt arrangement describes the impact on all parties involved. This may seem odd at first, but on a theoretical level, it creates a more complete economic model.

> A **debt arrangement** is the transfer of principal to another party with some agreement for repayment.
>
> A **credit market** is a social unit that is participating in debt arrangements.

An example of a village with a primitive economy illustrates the role of debt arrangements. Imagine a small village that does not use money. One day, one of the villagers is hungry for some food. The hungry villager approaches a neighbor who is good at the task of making food. There is not something readily available for exchange in barter, so the neighbor gives the food to the hungry villager. The preparer of the food makes a mental note that this villager owes him the value of one meal. The two parties have just created a debt arrangement. Sometime in the future the neighbor who provided the food can go to the other villager and make a request for some item or service, which will alter the outstanding amount of the debt.

Now imagine a more modern example: a customer taking their clothes to be dry-cleaned. It is easy to consider this a simple cash transaction, but what is really happening is that this person is creating a debt arrangement. By handing the dry cleaner cash in exchange for cleaning the clothes, the customer becomes in debt to the dry cleaner performing the service. The customer closes out the debt by paying cash at that moment. However, consider the true nature of cash. A dollar bill is really just an I.O.U. from the government for $1 of value. In our complex economy, you are closing out the dry cleaning debt, by providing another form of debt, which the dry cleaner can use to create another debt arrangement with someone else. Our transactions today are not so different from those of a primitive economy that does not use cash. Every transaction is a form of debt arrangement.

With the understanding that all transactions are debt arrangements, it is possible to create a theoretical model of credit markets. Imagine two individuals: x and y. They live in a defined theoretical environment and they initially divide the resources equally, so they begin with the same amount of assets. Suppose they are similar in all aspects except x is more productive than y. This information creates a set of assumptions (**Figure 2**).

ASSUMPTIONS (per period)

	Assets	FTE	Production
X	5	1	3
Y	5	1	-1

Figure 2. Credit market model assumptions.

An **asset** is a resource that is under an entity's control and contributes to production. Accountants define this term differently because they do not include all resources, like human capital, on company balance sheets. For the purpose of these economic models, human capital is included because it contributes to production.

Production is the value created during a given period. Some real world examples include production output less costs, revenue less expenses, or GDP for a country.

With assumptions established, we can begin running simulations. In the assumptions above, *x* is more productive each period. *Y* has greater costs than the ability to produce resulting in negative production. Each individual is one FTE (full-time equivalent) with an equal amount of assets. A simple computer simulation uses these assumptions to determine the outcome of this market over five periods. The computer creates two scenarios: one without any credit arrangements between the parties (**Figure 3**) and one with a credit arrangement (**Figure 4**). **(A description of the math used in these calculations is included in Appendix 1)**

TIMELINE

	0	1	2	3	4	5
X	$5.00	$8.00	$11.00	$14.00	$17.00	$20.00
Y	$5.00	$4.00	$3.00	$2.00	$1.00	$0.00
Total	$10.00	$12.00	$14.00	$16.00	$18.00	$20.00

Figure 3. Scenario 1 - No debt arrangement.

TIMELINE

	0	1	2	3	4	5
X	$8.99	$13.99	$18.99	$23.99	$28.99	$33.99
Y	$1.01	$2.01	$3.01	$4.01	$5.01	$6.01
Total	$10.00	$16.00	$22.00	$28.00	$34.00	$40.00

Figure 4. Scenario 2 - With debt arrangement.

These simulations reveal why credit markets work. In scenario 2, both parties are better off by entering into debt arrangements, and the total production of the group doubles by period five. In the first scenario, each party works alone and *y* ends up losing everything. The reason for the increase in wealth in scenario 2, is that assets transfer from *y* to *x*, and those assets are utilized by *x*'s higher productivity. *Y* shares in this additional wealth through debt payments. It is not a shocking concept to suggest that a group working together produces more than they would individually. What I am suggesting is an extension of that idea. Modeling a transaction as a debt arrangement is a way to calculate in financial terms the benefit of working together. The assets transfer from an area of lower productivity to an area of higher productivity creating additional wealth for the system. An economic model that only considers one perspective misses the group dynamics involved in debt.

The simulations also create accurate descriptions of real-life transactions. Re-examining the dry cleaning example, we find that the interaction fits the same characteristics from the simulations. The dry cleaner is more productive at dry cleaning than the customer is. The customer transfers assets to the dry cleaner in the form of cash. The dry cleaner will perform the service at their higher rate of productivity. Finally, the dry cleaner returns the value of the customer's initial investment back in the form of clean clothes. Since the transaction is instantaneous, there is no interest. In this case, everyone is significantly better off. The customer is better off because they utilize the dry cleaner's higher productivity. The dry cleaner is better off, because their internal costs are less than the value of the service, generating a profit. Another way to think of this situation is like the arrangement between the two villagers. Instead of paying cash for dry cleaning, the customer could have created a debt arrangement where the dry cleaner would perform the service and the customer would return the value later.

$$A_{N\,no\,cm} + (P_{cm} - P_{no\,cm}) * N = A_{N\,cm}$$
$$\$20 + (\$6 - \$2) * 5 = \$40$$

$$A_{N\,no\,cm} = Market\ Assets\ at\ period\ N\ with\ no\ credit\ market$$
$$A_{N\,cm} = Market\ Assets\ at\ period\ N\ with\ a\ credit\ market$$
$$P_{no\,cm} = Market\ Production\ with\ no\ credit\ market$$
$$P_{cm} = Market\ Production\ with\ a\ credit\ market$$
$$N = Number\ of\ periods$$

Figure 5. Equation describing the benefit from a debt arrangement.

A simple equation describes these market dynamics (**Figure 5**). This equation calculates the total increase in wealth between two entities by comparing productivity levels. The benefit of this equation is it enables us to calculate wealth creation in a social group from debt arrangements. This equation shows that a social unit that engages in credit markets is better off than a social unit that does not engage in credit markets.

High and low productivity

One benefit of modeling transactions as debt arrangements is that it describes power dynamics between participants in the credit market. Power dynamics form in favor of those with higher productivity. In this model, the person in debt is actually the more productive person in the relationship. Someone has lent money because that person can produce at a higher rate and share profits back with the lender through interest payments. The less productive is forming an agreement where they acknowledge a level of subservience to those with higher productivity. The less productive recognizes their lower ability, and gives away their assets. These actions give the highly productive person elevated status and power. Both parties need each other to increase the benefit for society, but the highly productive clearly has a more powerful position.

A common example of power dynamics is the employer/employee relationship. In a purely economic sense, the employee is less powerful than the business organization, because the employee is less productive. The employee makes an agreement to transfer 40 hours per week of their capacity to the employer. In return, the employer will make regular payments at a certain wage. The wage is equivalent to the value that employee is providing the business. From another perspective, the employee is an area of high productivity with regards to the use of the company's revenues. The cost of producing goods and services (building, supplies, raw materials, etc.) generate a higher production level with the employee rather than the business owner. So the employee transfers the asset of their time to produce with the business' resources. In other words, wages are being distributed to areas of lower productivity and assets are being controlled by areas of higher productivity. The business keeps as profit the difference between revenues and the cost to produce. This example shows all the elements of a credit market: the separation between high and low productivity, the formation of a debt arrangement, and the creation of wealth from the relationship.

Describing transactions in terms of power reveals that debt arrangements are actually net-zero events. It is easy to mistake debt payments as creation of value through interest. This is incorrect, because interest is not the creation of value, but the adjustment of a debt to account for the passage of time. The accounting supports the idea of debt as a net-zero event. The increase in cash (assets) is offset by the increase in payables (liabilities). The equity of the business remains unchanged.[3] Viewed from the market as a whole, debt arrangements are merely transferring assets from one party to another.

The cycle of debt provides a more accurate description of debt payments (**Figure 6**). For example, in a typical debt arrangement, one party transfers some large amount of principal up front and agrees to return the assets in small payments each period over some length of time. What occurs each period is a portion of the principal is used, and then an equivalent amount returns to the lender. The adjustment of interest is simply a way to take into account the element of time, so the value used is the same as the value paid. The debt payments themselves are a net-zero event and do not create any value. The movement of assets is what creates value, because the market uses them in an area of higher productivity.

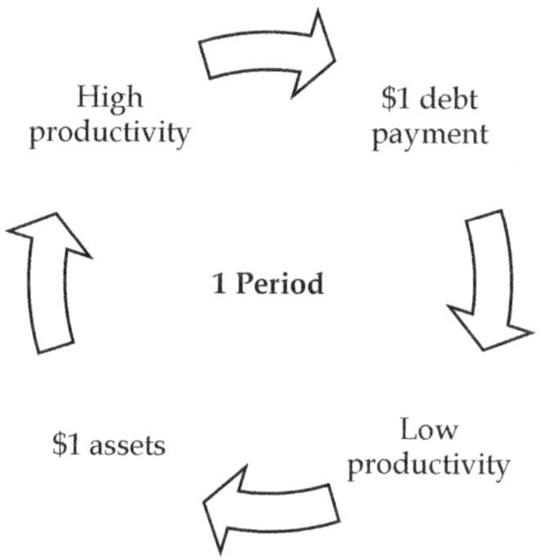

Figure 6. Cycle of debt.

To illustrate the usefulness of this model of power dynamics, we can consider one of the central questions of business, "why do societies have rich and poor?" This is a difficult question to ponder. The world has an enormous amount of income inequality. Of course, a large amount of social status comes from being born into a certain economic situation. However, this does not account for the enormous difference in wages around the world. We are essentially all human beings, and yet we select some individuals to pay significantly higher wages. For instance, imagine a pair of identical twins that work in separate careers. Their employers will likely pay each twin different wages, even though their biology and upbringing are the same. The difference in wages occurs because there is a difference in productivity. One of the twins is providing more utility to society in their role, and the contribution is valued at a higher wage.

Standard economic models do not explain the vast difference in income inequality. Income inequality is always a controversial subject to discuss, because it is difficult to calculate and can be interpreted in different ways. However, we can show that the gap between rich and poor has dramatically expanded over time since the industrial revolution.[4] In contrast, traditional economic theory suggests that competitive advantage in markets decreases over time. The "invisible hand" will allocate resources to areas with the lowest wages in order to generate the highest profit. However, over time, firms will enter industries that are generating abnormally high profit and increase the wages. Over the long run, incomes will reach a point of market equilibrium.[5] It is true that competitive advantage shrinks over time, but a model based on trends towards market equality does not explain the income inequality we experience today. We need a new approach that supports the idea of shrinking competitive advantage while explaining an increase in income inequality.

Debt arrangements provide a model that explains income inequality. In any group, the individuals will self-identify whether they are more or less productive. The difference in productivity incentivizes them to form debt arrangements, where the less productive individuals transfer assets to those who are more productive. In this way, everyone in the social unit is better off. This explains that wealth tends to move towards areas of higher productivity, which creates a discrepancy between rich and poor.

To illustrate these two approaches, imagine two individuals, *x* and *y*, living on a tropical island. One individual *x* owns the half of the island where all the coconut trees grow. Since individual *x* has the only access to coconuts, individual *x* charges a higher premium because supply is low. Traditional economic theory predicts that individual *y* will see the high profits from coconuts and decide to plant coconut trees on the other side of the island. Eventually, competition between *x* and *y* will bring down the price for coconuts, and incomes will eventually equalize. The alternative prediction from a model of debt arrangements suggests that individual *y* will give all his land to individual *x* in exchange for a portion of the profits through debt payments. This approach explains how huge income inequality occurs, because in a debt arrangement both individuals *x* and *y* are better off. It also does not contradict economic theory that still predicts shrinking competitive advantage over time. In this case, the coconuts are still distributed, but not by *y* going through the hard work of planting his own trees, but simply by *y* recognizing subservience to *x*'s greater productivity.

It is noteworthy that this model of debt arrangements does not place importance on cost of capital. Most business literature on debt arrangements focuses primarily on the cost of capital, because it is a significant factor when we view the transaction from one perspective. When viewed by the market as a whole, cost of capital does not matter. Since the cycle of debt is a net-zero event, the interest does not significantly impact economic models. We saw this affect in the timeline of Scenario 2 (**Figure 4**). The interest payments are included in the timeline, but no matter what interest rate is used, it does not affect the overall wealth of the group. We can see this affect in a sensitivity analysis of Scenario 2 (**Figure 7**). The chart shows that production and assets are significant drivers of wealth, but interest rate is not. This suggests a different approach from most academic research on credit markets that focuses on cost of capital. Instead, economic models should focus on production and assets, which are the real drivers in an economic system.

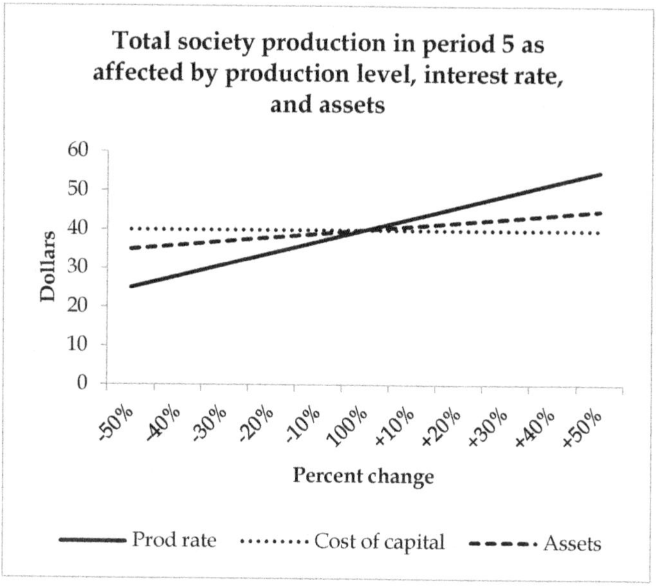

Figure 7. Sensitivity analysis of Scenario 2.

Group dynamics in credit markets

The previous examples only consider relationships between two individuals. If we extend the simulations to include multiple relationships, it reveals the common characteristics of credit markets. Computer simulations can include thousands of individuals over long periods. The results tell us who gains in wealth, what are the most significant variables, and how market dynamics change over time.

A common characteristic that always occurs in simulations of credit markets is that individuals quickly form communities. The individuals self-select themselves into higher or lower productivity categories and then transfer their assets. This quickly creates significant income inequality as groups form under the most productive individuals. Within each social group, the individual with the higher productivity utilizes the assets of the less productive. Not everyone chooses to participate in the credit market in the initial period. However, the production level within each credit market is so much higher, that it eventually dominates the entire community, incorporating all players somehow in debt arrangements.

Another common characteristic that occurs in simulations is that each community operates as a unified social unit. Even if the simulation contains many participants, you can effectively simplify the model by representing all the participants as one massively productive individual. In other words, the total assets of the community represent one FTE performing at the community's higher production rate. Market participants are no longer acting as individuals, but as a conglomerate.

Additional variables can make the simulation more realistic. One example is to add a changing variable for each person's "productivity," representing an individual's life cycle. A productivity life cycle is one way to portray individuals with more realistic assumptions (**Figure 8**). Most individuals start their lives with low production, relying on others to survive. Then individuals experience a period of greater productivity where they acquire assets. At some point, the individuals retire and their productivity decreases. During this final period, individuals create more value by living off debt payments from their assets rather than their own productivity. Both individuals and businesses experience this rise and fall in productivity. The interesting effect in simulations is that, even though the individual production levels rise and fall, the credit market as a whole tends to experience steady growth. This is similar to what we experience in real markets.

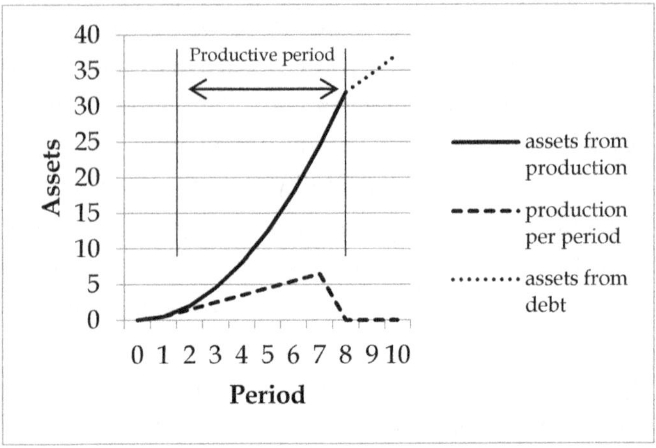

Figure 8. Individual productivity life cycle.

An example that illustrates the debt life cycle is the home mortgage and the reverse mortgage. In a mortgage agreement, there are two participants: the homeowner and the bank. The bank is the area of low productivity. This is opposite from how most people view banks, but it reflects the way credit markets actually function. The bank has a large number of assets that achieves a higher return by lending to others with higher productivity. The bank assumes the homeowner is the area of high productivity, and transfers the assets. The bank hopes the homeowner will create a higher return through some lucrative occupation or by improving the property and then returning the value back to the bank through debt payments. In a reverse mortgage, the homeowner is in a different part of the debt-life cycle. The homeowner is usually retired with the home completely paid off. In this situation, the homeowner becomes like the bank with low productivity and high assets. The homeowner transfers the assets to an area with higher productivity (usually with a bank acting as an intermediary), and receives value back through regular debt payments.

Another variable we can add to the simulation is "knowledge transfer." The benefit of an individual forming a debt arrangement with someone with higher productivity is that the lower productive individual gains access to more productive technology. Over time, the knowledge and skills transfer to the lower productive individual which increases their productive capacity. Given enough knowledge transfer, the less productive becomes an area of high productivity. In a simulation where knowledge transfer does not occur, one individual takes the social position of high productivity and usually remains for the entire simulation. However, by including a variable for knowledge transfer, the high productivity position in the credit market switches between individuals, depending on their ability to increase capacity.

The variable for knowledge transfer explains the concept of income mobility. Like income inequality, income mobility is a controversial issue. It is difficult to calculate and complicated by factors like inheritance. However, from an economic perspective, knowledge transfer explains how market power transfers to the individuals in society who produce the greatest value.

Scenario 2 illustrates the concept of income mobility (**Figure 4**). The scenario ends in period five with a significant gap in wealth among the market participants. Questions about income mobility ask, "What happens in period six?" Can the poor individual become rich, or does the economic system forever lock the individual into a position of poverty? The answer is... it depends.

Knowledge transfer determines what occurs in period six. If *y* successfully transfers knowledge during the previous five periods, then *y* enters period six with the same productivity as *x*. The productivity of *x* has actually decreased because it no longer experiences the benefits of a debt arrangement. X has the previous five periods to learn how to increase productivity or risks moving to low productivity compared to *y*. This example illustrates that even though credit markets encourage income inequality, income mobility is possible through knowledge transfer. Perhaps even more important, if knowledge transfer occurs, there is no guarantee that individual *x* stays in the highly productive position.

Another important insight on income mobility is the dilemma of poverty. A poverty line does exist in simulations that lock participants into a life of poverty. If an individual begins the simulation with both an extremely low level of assets and low productivity, it creates a point of no return. The debt payments from the assets are so small that they cannot cover the individual's costs each period. The downwards spiral towards losing everything traps the individual with no other options. This shows the extreme downside to low productivity.

In all of these different simulations, there are common characteristics that recur. The Theory of Inequality summarizes these characteristics and provides a general description of how credit markets work.

The Theory of Inequality

1. Whenever there is a group of two or more individuals, they will self-select into areas of high and low productivity
2. The difference in productivity creates a benefit to working together, and incentivizes individuals to form debt arrangements.

Period infinity

Another important insight provided by the Theory of Inequality is that market participants value different things depending on their position within the market. The earlier sensitivity analysis (**Figure 7**) shows that production and assets are the most important variables. What we observe when markets split into areas of high and low productivity is that high productivity areas only value *production*, while low productivity areas only value *assets*. This is because individuals with higher productivity create value from production, whereas individuals with lower productivity create value through assets. Different variations on the initial assumptions always produce the same dynamic.

To illustrate this concept, imagine what occurs in period infinity. If we expand a simulation into the future an infinite number of periods, assets will grow every period and eventually reach infinity. Debt payments from assets are also going to be infinity, plus a little bit more to account for interest. Assuming return on assets is any positive value, production is also infinity. In this scenario, all assets transfer to the highest area of productivity. All the output from production would transfer back to cover the enormous debt payment. In other words, high productivity is only concerned about production to make their debt payments. Low productivity is only concerned about assets because that is the source of their debt income.

Whether in period infinity or the current period, the same market dynamics play out through the cycle of debt. The assets in a system are transferring between areas of high and low productivity in the following sequence.

1. Areas of low productivity transfer assets to areas of high productivity.
2. Areas of high productivity produce with those assets.
3. At the end of the period, assets transfer back to areas of low productivity through debt payments.
4. The next period, the cycle repeats.

This understanding of the true drivers of credit markets suggests another type of model that represents the market as one entity and tracks the development of production and assets over time.

Figure 9 shows an example where each period the assets are used to purchase 1 FTE at the system's production level. Every period is a cycle of assets between low and high productivity. This same behavior takes place in business investment. An investor determines that some amount of cash (assets) will generate a higher return somewhere else. The investor purchases stock in a business that has higher productivity. Profits return to investors through dividends. This model illustrates what is occurring with production and assets as the main drivers of the credit market.

TIMELINE

	Period	0	1	2	3
Production	P	5	5	5	
Assets	A	1	6	11	16

Figure 9. Unified model of a credit market.

The history of money

Even though the Theory of Inequality provides useful information on market dynamics, many economists will find the approach problematic, because it challenges the generally accepted history of economics. Most economists describe the history of economic development in the following sequence.[6]

1. Individuals come together and begin bartering for goods and services.
2. Society invents money as legal tender and replaces barter.
3. Credit markets form to aid transactions.

However, the Theory of Inequality suggests economies developed in the opposite sequence, because it defines all transactions as debt arrangements. This suggests that credit markets developed very early in history before money. Whenever groups form, evolution would encourage participation in credit markets because of the vast increase in production. The invention of money and bartering occurs later and enhances the already established practice of debt arrangements.

Research in anthropology supports the idea that credit markets developed first. Anthropologists who study how economies have actually developed throughout history, as well as the few primitive economies that exist today, find that economies develop in the manner suggested by the Theory of Inequality. In these cases, credit markets develop first, then money, then barter. Scholar David Graeber explains in his book Debt: the First 5,000 Years:

> "The standard economic-history version has little to do with anything we observe when we examine how economic life is actually conducted. In real communities and market-places, almost anywhere- one is much more likely to discover everyone in debt to everyone else in a dozen different ways, and that most transactions take place without the use of currency."[7]

The research in anthropology shows that the idea of transactions as debt arrangements is much closer to the dynamics we find in real markets.

The Theory of Inequality redefines the role of money. Money is just a form of exchange. By itself, money does not really mean anything. It only represents the value of the underlying debt arrangement between two parties that are self-identifying themselves into different levels of productivity.

The wolves of Wall Street

At this point, it is helpful to take a step back and reflect on the characteristics of credit markets. It is curious that human interaction is not the only place we see these social dynamics. One intriguing example is that a pack of wolves exhibits a very similar power structure. In areas without human habitation, wolves are often the top of the food chain. Wolves, like humans, are pack animals and live in groups. Within the pack, one animal assumes the role of the alpha-dog, and the others are subservient. The alpha-dog fulfills the role of the highly productive in terms of physical strength, hunting ability, etc. These group dynamics based on productivity are an important driver of wolf behavior.

Dr. Simon Townsend performed a recent study of wolf howling patterns, which supports the idea of similarities between credit markets and wolf behavior. He explains, "Wolves seem to howl more when higher ranking individuals leave because these individuals play quite important roles in the social lives of wolves."[8] This is significant because it illustrates that wolves are not simply animals making noises. They are sending social signals based on the dominance rank of the other wolves. The social dynamics in the wolf pack are forming under the same financial calculations as human credit markets. The wolves are self-selecting themselves into categories of high and low productivity.

This example suggests that the Theory of Inequality is not only limited to humans, but may also describe interactions in biology as well. I do not claim to be an expert on biology or wolves, but it is not a stretch to see examples in nature with the same dynamics as human markets. My suggestion is that the differences between humans and the animal world may not be as great as we would like to think. If the Theory of Inequality suggests that credit markets developed very early in history, how early did they develop? Imagine Wall Street at a point in history before humans migrated to the area. Wolves would have dominated the area and interacted in market dynamics similar to what future Wall Street traders would experience. The Theory of Inequality suggests that the evolutionary process drives the formation of credit markets, which affects all areas of biology. In other words, capitalism is in our DNA.

A flexible capital structure

The Theory of Inequality can provide better understanding of a number of business issues. Determining an appropriate capital structure is one of the difficult questions faced by many business professionals. The previous examples suggest that individuals maximize their utility by entering into as much debt as possible. Practical application for business is more complex, because higher levels of debt create greater risk. At some point, there should be an optimal balance between value added from debt and an appropriate level of risk. Academic research has provided a number of tools that are helpful, but there is no consensus on the best method to identify the optimal capital structure. This creates ambiguity for business professionals. Many understand the benefits of debt, but have difficulty determining the correct ratio of debt to equity.

The current methods of choosing capital structure rely heavily on credit ratings. Credit rating agencies play a central role in influencing debt decisions. The rating agency determines a rating for a company based on a combination of statistical models and the judgment of the rating committee. These ratings determine an entity's "credit," which affects the amount businesses can borrow at a certain interest rate. Businesses rely on these ratings in making capital structure decisions. A business will balance the decision of whether to issue debt by considering the impact to their credit rating.[9]

It is easy to misinterpret the role of credit rating agencies in determining capital structure. The rating given by the agencies is not what creates a company's "credit." Credit is a function of the true drivers in credit markets: production and assets. Capital structure decisions that target a specific percentage of debt/equity are focusing on the wrong question. The more accurate question is whether an increase in debt will improve production or assets with reliable cash flows. Of course, businesses cannot ignore the established credit rating system, but theoretically, this model provides additional insight. If the company increases productivity or grows assets, the credit rating should adjust accordingly.

The other consideration for capital structure decisions is the business environment. Just like in market simulations, businesses observe their environment and determine areas of high and low productivity. Businesses want debt arrangements with others who have low productivity relative to the organization, because the company can use their assets to increase production. Businesses also want to form debt arrangements with those who have higher productivity, because it allows for knowledge transfer and provides sources of income. Understanding the business environment is a function of where the business falls in the continuum of low to high productivity compared to its peers. If there are many areas of lower productivity compared to the business, the business wants to increase debt by entering into as many debt arrangements as possible. If there are not any opportunities to use other's assets in debt arrangements that suggests the company has lower productivity relative to its environment. The business is better off deleveraging and investing funds in areas of higher productivity. This also illustrates the power dynamics in the credit market, because the more productive entities will be able to carry more debt.

The Theory of Inequality suggests that businesses should make capital structure decisions in a two-step process. This is similar to the Internal/External process in a SWOT strategic analysis (Strengths, Weaknesses, Opportunities, and Threats).[10] However, the following approach focuses specifically on assets and production as economic drivers.

1. **Internal analysis:** Determine assets and production for the business. As long as cash flows are *reliable,* additional debt will increase value.
2. **External analysis:** Compare assets and production for your peers. Forming debt arrangements appropriately with areas of low and high productivity will increase value.

Using this model, capital structure is flexible reflecting the dynamics of each particular credit market.

A simple example that illustrates this approach is the debt arrangement between two farmers. Imagine two farms, and each farm is worth $10M. However, "farmer *x*" is more productive and yields 100 units of crops per period whereas "farmer *y*" only produces 75 units of crops per period. Assume that farmer *x* uses crop futures, which guarantees the cash flow from crops to remove risk from this example. Farmer *y* would maximize utility by transferring everything he owns to the more productive farmer for a set period. In exchange, farmer *y* would work on the more productive farm and farmer *x* could improve the less productive farm so that it produces at the higher level of output. At the end of the contract, both farmers will have more wealth under this arrangement.

The example of the farmers reveals that capital structure is flexible. Even though both farms are in the same industry, they have two different capital structures. The typical accounting approach would record the debt arrangement as shown in the following table (**Figure 10**). The more productive farmer has more assets and more debt. However, the equity of both farmers remains at $10M. Additionally, if there were more opportunities to form agreements with less productive farms, assets for farmer *x* would continue to increase by adding more debt. There is not one correct ratio of debt to assets, but rather capital structure is a function of the internal and external factors driving the credit market.

	Farmer X	Farmer Y
Assets		
Accounts Receivable	0	10
Land	20	0
Debt		
Accounts Payable	10	0
Equity	10	10
Debt/Equity ratio	1	0

Figure 10. Balance sheet of two farmers.

Boom and bust

The Theory of Inequality can also provide insight on another business issue: why do we keep experiencing the peaks and valleys of the business cycle? It is surprising how recessions continue to take society by surprise, and every recession investors lose significant amounts of money. Investors are not good at predicting changes between bull and bear markets. When bear markets occur, panic affects decision-making, and the market acts irrationally. Simulations based on economic theories with rational players never display this kind of irrational activity. However, simulations using the Theory of Inequality can replicate similar market conditions.

These simulations suggest that the *reliability* of cash flows is the driver of recessions. We all exist in an uncertain universe, and cash flows have some amount of variance. When the variables for production levels in simulations include this variance, the simulations follow cycles of boom and bust like a real economy. In contrast, if cash flows were 100% certain, cycles of boom and bust would not occur and parties would not default on their debt arrangements.

An example of a farmer illustrates how the Theory of Inequality describes a market bubble. Imagine this farmer usually yields four units of crops per FTE per period. One year, the weather is abnormally good, and the farmer's yield increases from four units to ten. The farmer's assets for the following period are much higher than anticipated; the farmer is experiencing a boom period. In fact, the farmer might start to think the farm's capacity to produce is much higher than previously thought. The credit market incentivizes the farmer to enter into debt arrangements based on the higher production levels. When the weather in the following period returns to normal, yield once again reduces to four units. The farmer cannot pay the debt and defaults (**Figure 11**).

ASSUMPTIONS

Production 4

Assets 1

TIMELINE

Period	0	1	2	3
P	4	10	[10]	
A	1	5	15	[25]

Figure 11. Timeline of a farmer in a market bubble.

ASSUMPTIONS

Production 4

Assets 1

TIMELINE

Period	0	1	2	3
P	4	10	[4]	
A	1	5	15	[19]

Figure 12. Timeline of a farmer avoiding a market bubble.

This timeline suggests that the variance in cash flows will create boom and bust cycles. Market dynamics incentivize individuals to form as many debt arrangements as possible. When external factors create a temporary positive variance, it is easy to mistake the higher production level as reliable. Unrealistically high assumptions of future production levels result in people taking on too much debt. The result is an unusually high number of people defaulting on their debt arrangements, which causes the recession. In other words, the bust period is not the problem; it is the boom period. This reveals how important risk management is within a business. Risk management can accurately identify variances in cash flows and determine how much debt to use. This information becomes part of capital structure decisions. To continue the example of the farmer, if the farmer identifies the increase in cash flow as unreliable, the farmer avoids taking on additional debt (**Figure 12**). In this case, the business avoids the boom and bust cycle.

A new framework

The Theory of Inequality provides a new framework that is helpful in making business decisions. Simulations based on these concepts create computerized credit markets that display the same market dynamics we see in real markets. These theoretical universes provide clues to rethink some of the basic economic principles that drive business. On a practical level, the ability to describe situations in terms of assets and production encourages users to identify the root economic drivers and make appropriate strategic decisions.

The Theory of Inequality also provides a deeper understanding that credit markets are a collection of relationships. Any market derives its strength from the individual parties working together. One person working alone is not very effective, even if that person has incredibly high productivity. An individual with lesser productivity who effectively leverages relationships will outperform anyone working alone. The world economy is a complex web of debt arrangements. Each debt arrangement is a relationship, and together we form a credit market of incredible power and limitless potential.

PART II: THE PULL OF DEBT

Understanding growth

Business executives often discuss the subject of growth, however there is no accepted explanation of why growth occurs. Growth is all around us. Growth occurs in long-run trends in most economic activity. Throughout human history, from cave dwellers to skyscrapers, society as a whole has continued to grow. Even in economies that are not growing, it is usually because growth has moved to continue somewhere else. Of course, there are examples of specific civilizations that have collapsed, but humanity as a whole experiences growth. Individual businesses also provide examples of rising and falling economic activity, but the economy overall generally experiences growth. Growth could even be considered a universal aspect of economic activity. We know that we like growth and want more of it, and yet we do not fully understand it. However, if we model transactions as credit markets, the model explains the phenomenon of growth.

Economists have never agreed on an understanding of growth, because the concept is in conflict with generally accepted economic theory. Most economists believe that markets reach a point of equilibrium. If that were the case, once a market reaches equilibrium, why would it continue to grow? Changing conditions in the environment would not account for continued growth. Some suggest that population growth might explain economic growth, but economies have always grown much faster than population. Some relate growth to increases in technology, but new technology is merely the result of investment decisions. A more critical question is why does technology investment continue to grow? Achieving growth is expensive, so it is unclear why economies grow at all.

To develop a definition of growth, it is necessary to describe what we see in actual economies. **Figure 13** shows a chart of US GDP from 1950 – 2010.[11] Over this period, economic activity shows consistent exponential growth. In fact, the GDP curves of all nations show a similar pattern of exponential growth.

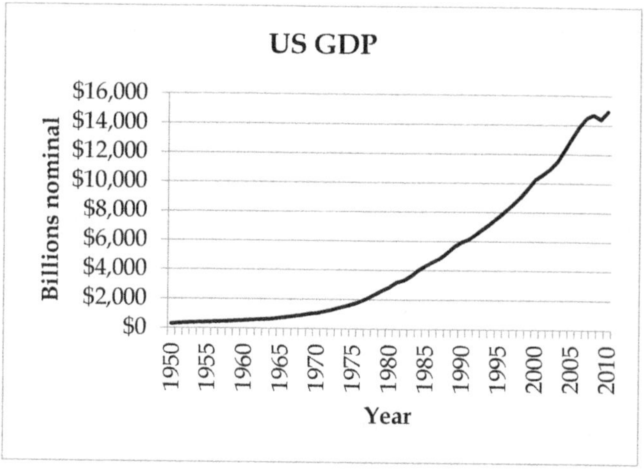

Figure 13. US GDP 1950-2010. Data from U.S. Bureau of Economic Analysis

Examples of economic growth reveal that growth patterns tend to form in a specific type of parabola shape. Most standard economic models differ from this example by forecasting growth with a *constant growth* rate. However, I propose that *constant acceleration* better describes this parabola shape. Constant acceleration is something that we know how to model from physics because the forces of gravity follow a similar parabola shape. A parabola is a conic section created by drawing a plane through a cone. Different parabola shapes result depending on where the plane intersects the cone. In the case of economic data, the parabola shape that occurs is similar to a parabola shape that frequently appears in nature when objects travel with constant acceleration. For example, a ball bouncing against the constant force of gravity travels with constant acceleration. This occurs because the Earth's gravitational pull is a constant of 9.8 m/s^2. If someone were to drop an object, a chart of that object's position in the fall over time would form a parabola as it travels faster every second.[12] This same methodology can be useful to understanding the parabola shapes in growth charts.

This description of growth is in conflict with many financial equations. As already mentioned, finance professionals usually hold growth constant, rather than hold acceleration constant. Holding growth constant forecasts a series of cash flows that increase by that constant percentage every period (**Figure 14**). This is the most commonly used approach to forecast cash flows and generates a different type of parabola shape.

$$FCF_1, FCF_{N-1}(1+g), FCF_{N-1}(1+g) \ldots$$
$$FCF = Free\ Cash\ Flow$$
$$N = Number\ of\ Period$$
$$g = growth\ rate$$

Figure 14. Equation for cash flows that increase by a constant growth rate (g).

It may seem esoteric to argue over which variable to hold constant. However, the difference is quite significant. **Figure 15** contrasts the two methods of forecasting cash flows over 10 periods. At first glance, this may not appear to make much difference in the parabola shapes.

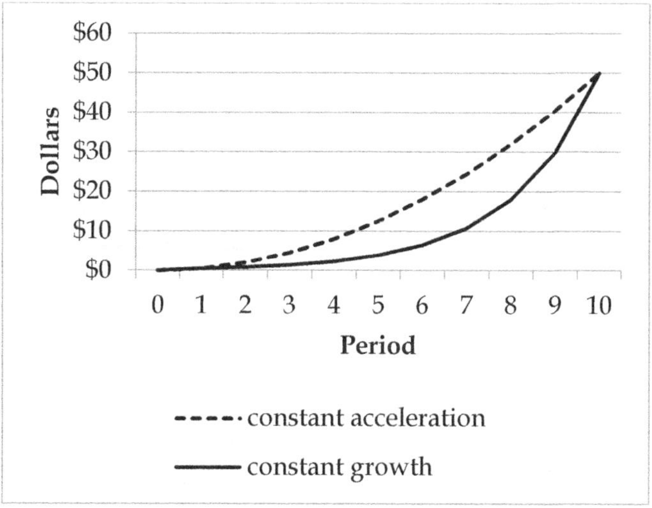

Figure 15. Comparison of the two different forecasting methods (10 periods).

Over more extended periods, the differences become far more significant. **Figure 16** extends the time line to twenty periods. It is clear that these methods suggest very different parabola shapes, and very different representations of economic activity.

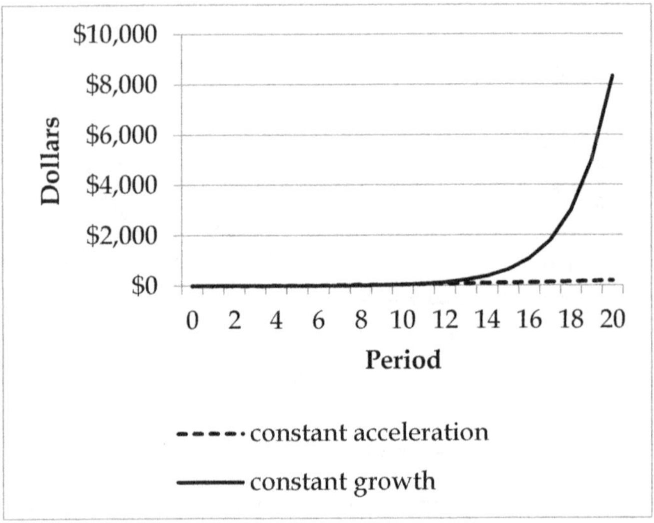

Figure 16. Comparison of the two different forecasting methods (20 periods).

The equation for constant acceleration helps to understand the differences between these two methods of forecasting growth. The equation for constant acceleration uses the two variables *F* and N^2. The variable *F* describes the amount of constant acceleration each period while the variable N^2 describes how much of that acceleration has occurred depending on the period in time. These two variables work together to create the exponential growth parabola shape.

The physics equation for the constant acceleration experienced under the force of gravity can also be adapted to describe the constant acceleration experienced in economic activity. **Figure 17** uses the equation for the position of a falling object, but replaces the constant for gravity with a different constant defined as "*F*." This constant is the force describing the level of fertility in the system. This book discusses the variable *F* in more detail in Part III. What is important here is that *F* interacts with the variable N^2 to describe a parabola shape under constant acceleration. To use a simple example, **Figure 18** defines *F* as $1 and the starting position as $0. This equation produces a beautiful parabola as the curve accelerates at a constant force of $1 per period. This shape is also strikingly similar to the exponential growth in the U.S. GDP curve. This understanding of growth raises an interesting question: What if there is some constant force pulling the economy up?

$$y_1 = y_0 + \frac{1}{2}FN^2$$

$$y_1 = ending\ amount;\ y_0 = starting\ amount;$$
$$F = level\ of\ fertility;\ N = number\ of\ periods$$

Figure 17. Equation for constant acceleration in economic activity.

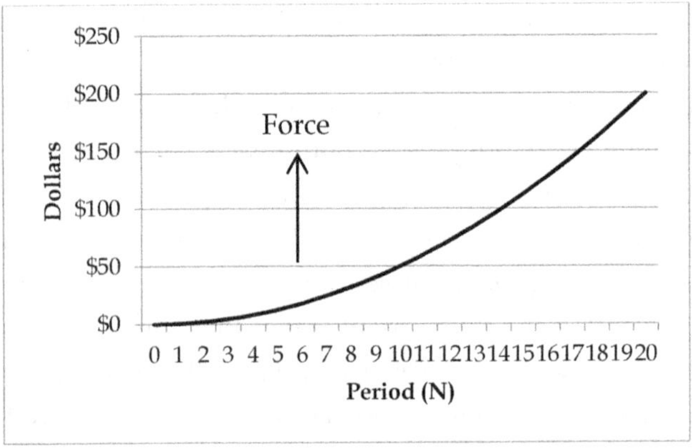

Figure 18. Graph of constant acceleration of $1.

The benefit to creating growth curves using constant acceleration rather than constant growth is that it creates a more realistic forecast because the variable for growth (g) decreases every period. This is much more in line with our experience of growth in real markets. The larger an organization grows, the more difficult it becomes to maintain the same growth rate. In other words, it is easier to double the size of a $1 Million company, than it is to double the size of a $1 Billion company. The faster the economy moves, the heavier it becomes.

Examples from real economic data show the phenomenon of decreasing growth rates over time. Gradually decreasing growth over time produces much more realistic forecasts. **Figure 19** shows the decreasing growth rate of U.S. GDP over the last 50 years. [13] This conflicts with the common method of using a constant rate for growth. Of the two methods, using a constant variable for acceleration provides a description of growth that is much closer to our experience in real markets.

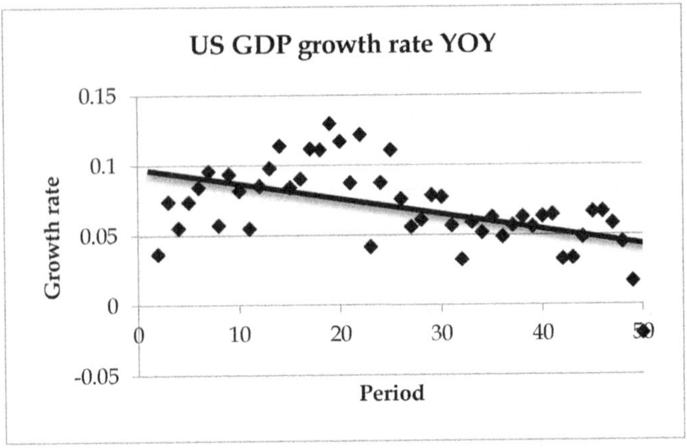

Figure 19. US GDP growth rate YOY. Data from U.S. Bureau of Economic Analysis.

These examples identify four characteristics of growth that we commonly find in economic data.

Growth

1. Growth occurs in economic markets
2. Growth occurs exponentially
3. Growth occurs with constant acceleration
4. When growth does not occur within a defined market, the growth has moved to continue in another market.

Insurance

A definition for growth is helpful, but it does not provide any insight into why growth occurs in this manner. Of all the possible ways to grow, why do economies grow with constant acceleration? Why do we all have the urge to grow and improve ourselves when it is much easier to spend the time relaxing? Surely, we produce enough goods as a species to slow down our exponential growth curve. The reason for growth remains elusive. However, the evidence in economic data suggests that growth is speeding up with constant acceleration. Closer examination of the equation for constant acceleration provides some compelling insights into the purpose of growth.

Of all the possible ways economic activity could develop, constant acceleration is a very robust way to grow. From a mathematical perspective, the new growth created each period is incrementally more than the previous period. This incremental growth provides protection against unexpected changes in future cash flows in direct proportion to the size and complexity of the social unit. In other words, constant acceleration creates "insurance" each period that is necessary for survival in an uncertain environment.

This definition of systemic insurance expands the traditional concept of insurance. Finance defines insurance using option pricing that values volatility in cash flows over a defined period.[14] This definition makes sense when evaluating a cash flow from one perspective. However, when viewing that same cash flow from a system's perspective, there is another component. The larger the credit market that cash flow occurs in, the lower the risk to the system. The opposite is also true: the smaller the credit market that cash flow occurs in, the higher the risk. This additional definition of insurance describes the system's ability to absorb the shock in the event the cash flow defaults. The traditional concept of insurance does not capture this market dynamic, which is a useful definition in describing a credit market.

Three main ideas support the concept of growth functioning as a form of insurance. The first is that what we observe matches the concept of systemic insurance. We have seen that as an organization grows larger, its growth rate decreases. This matches the idea that as an organization grows larger, its systemic risk decreases. For instance, a few individuals living in isolation have a greater risk of system collapse than a large and complex society does. The large society reacts better when debt arrangements default, because another debt arrangement can take its place. Therefore, it is reasonable to assume that a system, depending on its size and complexity, has an inherent level of risk, and growth that matches the need for insurance will be the most productive way to grow over time.

To use an example, imagine a social unit of only three entities: a bank, a farm, and a distributor. No entity trades with anyone outside of the social unit. At the beginning of a period, each entity makes credit arrangements with each other based on expected production by the end of the period. If any one of the entities fails to realize their expected cash flows, it is devastating to the other parties within the system. However, imagine a social unit of 30 entities that is a combination of banks, farms, and distributors. If one entity fails, it is a much smaller impact and therefore less risky.

A comparison of large and small companies is another example. Procter & Gamble has less systemic risk than a small start-up company would. Even a division within Procter & Gamble with the same characteristics and cash flow as the individual small start-up company has less systemic risk. The Procter & Gamble division exists within a larger and more complex organization. This allows the division to withstand unexpected economic impacts.

The second main idea supporting the concept of growth as a form of insurance is that the equation for constant acceleration provides a mathematical explanation for systemic insurance. To show how the equation achieves this effect, **Figure 20** illustrates the equation's growth over time. For simplicity, the variable "*F*" is equal to one. Imagine each "*D*" as standing for one unit of debt ($.50). Also, remember the concept that assets and debt within a system are related concepts. Debt represents the assets that circulate among the parties each period. Think of this diagram as the growing quantity of debt (or assets) in the market.

1 D .50
2 D D D D 2.00
3 D D D D D D D D D 4.50
4 D D D D D D D D D D D D D D D D 8.00

Figure 20. Growth of debt over time.

Figure 20 shows the rate of new growth each period accelerating by the constant of *F* ($1). To make this concept clear, **Figure 21** circles the new growth each period. This feature of growth forms what I call the "Pyramid of Success."

1 D .50
2 D D D D 2.00
3 D D D D D D D D D 4.50
4 D D D D D D D D D D D D D D D D 8.00

Figure 21. Growth of debt over time showing the Pyramid of Success.

Showing how the Pyramid of Success develops reveals how this pattern performs the function of insurance. Consider new growth in period two (three units of debt as shown in **Figure 22**). Period one grew by one unit of debt (from nothing to one unit). So this market would feel confident in making debt arrangements to grow the same amount the following period. However, both parties grow by an additional unit, creating insurance equal to "*F*" ($1).

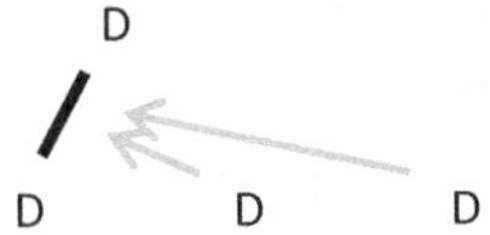

Figure 22. Growth of new debt in period two.

This process repeats the following period. In the new period, the system is more complex and requires less insurance proportional to the overall system (**Figure 23**). The arrows in the diagram show, how a unit of debt in a complex system could insure a contract that defaults. The curious aspect of this equation is that no matter what constant we assign for "*F*," growth along this curve will generate a changing level of insurance that reflects the changing systemic risk of the market.

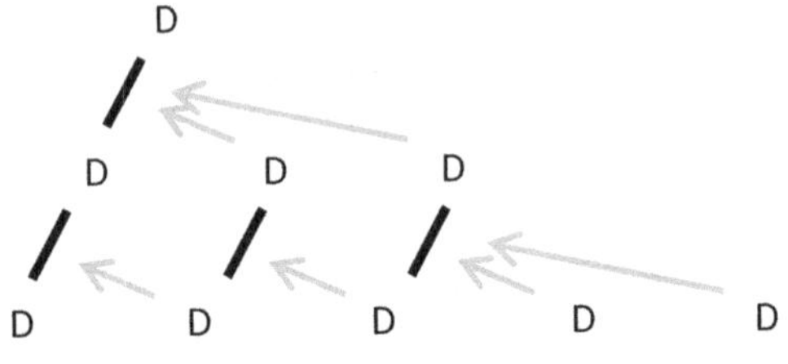

Figure 23. Growth of new debt in period three.

The third main idea supporting the concept of growth as insurance is that it explains why this particular pattern of growth evolved to become the dominant form of economic activity. People have the choice to grow at different growth rates. However, those who grow at a rate appropriate to the required amount of systemic insurance will make the most effective use of their resources. Over time, markets will tend to reflect the growth patterns of those who are using their resources effectively because the most productive will eventually dominate the market.

For example, imagine three individuals with the same amount of assets. One has the right amount of insurance. One purchases more insurance than is needed, and the other purchases less insurance than is needed. The two people using incorrect amounts of insurance are losing money. The person with too much insurance wastes funds on insurance and never uses it, and the person with too little insurance wastes funds when something bad occurs that is not covered. The individual who appropriately matches insurance to their risk will outperform over time, as they have the most effective use of their resources. The same phenomenon would be true of organizations that grow at a rate appropriate to their level of risk. Those organizations dominate, and markets tend towards the pattern of constant acceleration that we find in economic activity.

Another way to view this model of insurance is through the perspective of the VP of a company division. Imagine the VP's division grew by a certain amount in a period. The VP created that growth with the assets provided by the company's investors. If the investors return those assets for the following period, the investors expect the VP to perform the same feat and grow the division by the same amount. However, the uncertainty of the system incentivizes the VP to increase growth by a little extra for insurance. The VP grows the company at constant acceleration, because the amount of insurance generated balances the risk of the division at the size and complexity it achieves for that period.

These three reasons suggest that if growth occurs, it tends to use constant acceleration. It matches the conceptual definition of how systems experience risk. The equation for constant acceleration explains how growth matches the need for insurance. Finally, the proper use of insurance explains how this form of growth dominates the market. Systemic insurance achieves the same goals as the traditional concept of insurance: an additional outflow of value reduces future risk.

I refer to this phenomenon as the **Pull of Debt** which describes what growth is and why it occurs. Growth occurs in any system of debt arrangements because a decreasing growth rate is the most productive way to develop.

The Pull of Debt

1. transactions are really debt arrangements
2. debt arrangements are based on future cash flows
3. future cash flows involve uncertainty
4. the most productive way to grow under uncertainty is with insurance that appropriately matches the credit market's ability to handle risk
5. growth that occurs with constant acceleration matches the need for systemic insurance based on a market's size and complexity

The pull of debt does more than suggest an explanation for growth. It ties together the idea of growth with the Theory of Inequality. A more thorough understanding of growth allows us to build these growth patterns into economic simulations and achieve very realistic results. Part I discussed how the transfer of assets from areas of low productivity to high productivity create debt arrangements. Most debt arrangements have a time dimension and that introduces uncertainty. Uncertainty requires insurance, which is why the pull of debt leads to economic growth. Growth is the way debt arrangements translate into prosperity.

Credit markets in art history

"The second vice is lying; the first is running in debt."
– Benjamin Franklin

It is unfair to discuss the benefits of debt arrangements without discussing the dark side of debt, as is often portrayed in art and cultural expression throughout history. Mathematics describes debt from an analytical perspective, but art tells us how we *feel* about debt. Stories, plays, religious texts, and other cultural expressions consistently portray debt with a negative connotation. Shakespeare's famous play, "The Merchant of Venice" tells the story of the moneylender, Shylock, attempting to claim "a pound of flesh" as payment from the lead protagonist who defaulted on a loan. The Bible also is full of language about debt. The Bible takes the concept of "redemption" directly from the language of ancient finance.[15] In fact, one could interpret the Bible as a story about a debt arrangement, with the crucifixion redeeming the debt from the original sin in the Garden of Eden. In this way, the Bible links the concept of debt directly to the ideas of sin and guilt. These are just a few of the numerous examples of debt portrayed as inherently evil and bad. This theme is so common, because most people in society can relate to negative feelings about debt to some degree.

To understand debt, we need a definition that explains the negative feelings displayed in art history. Debt represents future cash flows that are uncertain. That uncertainty often causes stress. Every day we face unpredictable circumstances, from natural disasters to global financial collapse. Everyone knows someone who has had difficulty making a debt payment or who unexpectedly lost a source of income. No one can predict the future, but we base our debt arrangements on some forecast of future cash flows. Stress is what makes everyone uncomfortable.

These negative reactions to debt raises an important question: If we all hate debt so much, why do we keep entering into more and more debt every year? This question defines the ongoing conflict of debt. We enter into debt because analytically the benefits say debt is good. However, emotionally the uncertainty creates stress. I do not suggest that stress from uncertainty drives growth. Rather, I suggest that growth will occur whether we stress over it or not, because it is the most efficient use of resources. Stress is merely our awareness of uncertainty. Life can be scary, and humanity has developed stress as a biological response to uncertainty. However, the negative feelings of stress are only part of the dual nature of economic development. We experience the negatives of uncertainty over future debt payments followed by the positives of improved productivity. Art is our way of processing the conflict between the positives and negatives of ongoing economic development.

This emotional conflict in debt has become an engrained part of human experience. The example of language shows how we even talk in terms of debt. A simple exchange of "thank you" is very revealing about the underlying interaction. The meaning of the phrase "thank you" is most apparent in the Portuguese translation, *obrigado,* which derives from the more formal phrase "much obliged." When you say "thank you," you are actually saying, "I am in your debt." The French translation, *merci,* derives from mercy and is even more obvious. You are putting yourself in the position of a criminal begging for mercy to the benefactor holding your debt.[16]

Consider the simple exchange at a dinner table of asking for salt. By saying, "Please pass me the salt," you are really initiating a debt arrangement. Each party could act as independent agents and retrieve the salt themselves, but the group understands that it is the most productive if the person nearest the salt performs the pass. If you are not convinced this interaction classifies as a debt arrangement, consider what would happen if an individual did not pass the salt. The requestor would be furious. The reason is that the request forms an implicit agreement. By requesting the salt, the receiver agrees to pass the salt back at some point in the future. The simple pleasantry of "thank you" solidifies this agreement, while adding the subtext of negative feelings associated with being indebted to another person. Of course, the exchange ends with positive feelings from a delicious meal made salty with the least amount of effort.[17]

The subtext of debt arrangements makes the simple question of asking for salt filled with conflict. On the one hand, we realize the mathematical benefits of debt and want to enter into as much debt as possible. On the other hand, debt makes us feel uncomfortable and we dislike the idea of debt. This simple exchange shows humanity's deep understanding of transactions as debt. The pull of debt creates a definition of growth that fits, not only the mathematical explanation of debt, but our feelings about debt as well.

An alternate universe

A model of growth based on credit markets can explain market movements in a wide range of economic scenarios. This is unlike many financial models that only explain growth under very specific market conditions. A universal definition of growth should be more expansive. We can test this idea by setting up different simulations. Even if the simulations use different assumptions, we will see that the pull of debt can still interpret the results.

For example, let us consider how the pull of debt would function in a setting with additional constraints. So far, this book has discussed the pull of debt functioning in human economies without constraints. Supply and demand are unbounded, and the production rate is set where it generates the greatest amount of value. However, an environment could exist where the production rate is not set at the intersection of supply and demand, but rather, individuals give up value based on some constraint. Consider an economy where assets spoil. There is no incentive to grow in a way that creates more assets than will be used. Also, consider that new growth relies on the presence of a certain amount of assets. For instance, this would reflect a society that is heavily reliant on procreation for growth. Parents would need a certain amount of assets to support their children.

To create this simulation, we need to establish a set of additional constraints on the growth of production rates. Under such assumptions, individuals determine their production rate based on available assets, rather than their ability to grow. Too fast of growth and there would not be enough assets to support the new growth, causing new babies to die. Too slow of growth and unused production would not be used because assets spoil. Growth in this more constrained environment does not follow the curve of the pull of debt. The constraints stop the growth from following the natural tendency towards constant acceleration.

The simulation uses equations to describe the additional constraints. To build these constraints we can use the same methodologies as before and track the growth of production and assets over time. We understand the quantity of assets each period equals the previous assets plus the production rate of the previous period. These equations will only allow growth in production to occur in proportion to growth in assets (**Figure 24**). We derive the following equations and the sample timeline (**Figure 25**) using a value of five for both production and assets in the starting period. The chart (**Figure 26**) compares predicted growth under the pull of debt, with the growth achieved under the constraints.

$$A_N = P_{N-1} + A_{N-1}$$
$$P_N = P_{N-1} + A_N$$

Figure 24. Equations for constraints on production growth.

TIMELINE

	Period	0	1	2	3	4
Production	**P**	5	15	40	105	275
Assets	**A**	5	10	25	65	170

Figure 25. Timeline of simulation under constraints.

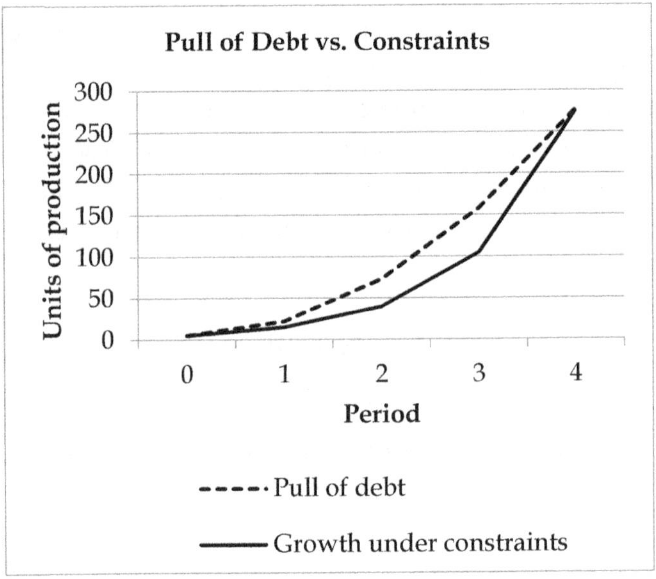

Figure 26. Graph of simulation under constraints.

In this simulation, growth is following constant growth rather than constant acceleration as described by the pull of debt. However, using constant acceleration as a benchmark enables an analysis that explains this growth pattern. These constraints describe the one scenario where Return on Assets (ROA) stays the same each period. This is different from a human economy where ROA changes each period because there is no constraints on assets. However, in this case, it is more important for this organization to achieve a growth rate in line with assets then it is to maximize growth. If we assume the pull of debt still holds true, in order for the entity to achieve the growth rate in the final period, it most likely was giving up potential growth in previous periods where it could have grown using constant acceleration. In the chart above, the entity is giving up 22% in value in order to grow with constant growth. This is the cost of the constraints. We see that even in simulations of bizarre growth patterns, the pull of debt provides a deeper understanding of the market.

This book does not attempt to explain that growth always follows the pull of debt. Rather, it suggests that economic activity has a tendency towards the pull of debt, unless there is some constraint. A continued examination of this scenario will further illustrate growth under these different incentives. Using the above equations, we can predict the growth of production and assets for any period in the future by simple substitution (**Figure 27**).

$$P_1 = P_0 + P_0 + A_0$$
$$P_2 = P_0 + P_0 + A_0 + P_0 + P_0 + A_0 + P_0 + A_0$$
$$P_3 = P_0 + P_0 + A_0 + P_0 + P_0 + A_0 + P_0 + A_0 + P_0 + P_0 + A_0 \ldots$$
$$+P_0 + P_0 + A_0 + P_0 + A_0 + P_0 + P_0 + A_0 + P_0 + A_0$$

Figure 27. Equations for production levels in any future period.

These equations simplify as follows (**Figure 28**).

$$P_1 = 2P_0 + A_0$$
$$P_2 = 5P_0 + 3A_0$$
$$P_3 = 13P_0 + 8A_0$$
$$P_4 = 34P_0 + 21A_0$$

Figure 28. Simplification of equations for production levels in any future period.

Do you see the pattern?...

The equations include a pattern known as Fibonacci numbers. In the middle ages, a mathematician named Leonardo Fibonacci was born in the Italian city of Pisa and made a significant contribution to the world of business. This was around the same time the city built the bell tower that we now know as the "Leaning Tower of Pisa." At that time, merchants were recording transactions using Roman numerals. For instance, someone using Roman numerals writes the number 1,246 as MCCXLVI. If you can imagine, it is quite difficult to record transactions or perform complex computations using Roman numeral notation. Fibonacci, who had done some traveling, brought back to Italy the concept of Arabic numbers (0, 1, 2, 3, 4...). He wrote a number of texts and advocated the practical use of Arabic numbers instead of Roman numerals. Of course, this was a significant benefit to the business community.[18]

Today we best remember Fibonacci for a number sequence he developed in the year 1202 known as the Fibonacci numbers. In a Fibonacci sequence, each number is the sum of the preceding two numbers. The Fibonacci sequence is 0, 1, 1, 2, 3, 5, 8, 13, 21, 34, 55, 89, 144, etc. **Figure 29** depicts this by drawing a spiral within squares whose sides are the length of the Fibonacci number sequence.[19]

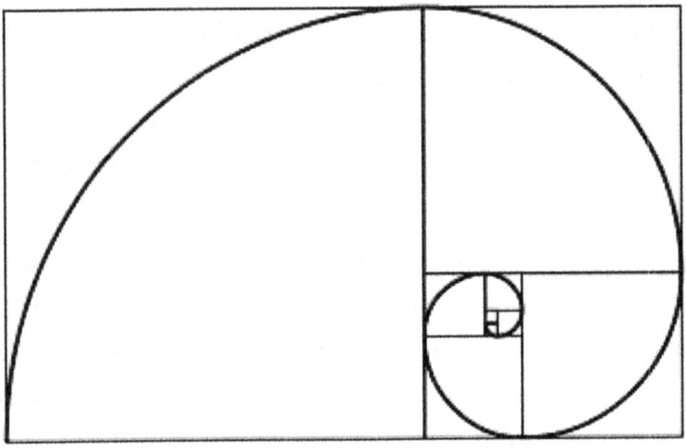

Figure 29. A spiral based on the Fibonacci number series.

The reason why Fibonacci numbers appear in the equations in **Figure 28** is that the constraints describe the proportions in the golden ratio. Fibonacci numbers appear whenever the golden ratio is in use. The equations used in the constraints are simply explaining that the proportion of the parts P and A grow in proportion with the whole $P+A$ (**Figure 30**).[20]

$$\frac{P+A}{P} = \frac{P}{A}$$

Figure 30. Proportions under simulation constraints.

By definition this is the same as the golden ratio, as represented by the Greek letter φ (Phi). Both the growth rate and return on assets is φ for each period (**Figure 31**).[21]

$$\frac{a+b}{a} = \frac{a}{b} = \varphi = 1.6180339887\ldots$$

Figure 31. Equation for the golden ratio.

This sequence has captured the imagination of mathematicians, because Fibonacci numbers show themselves repeatedly in nature. There is an enormous body of work in mathematics about the golden ratio and Fibonacci numbers. Scientists have found Fibonacci spirals in pinecones, sunflowers, cactus and many other examples.[22]

Biologists do not yet have an explanation why nature organizes itself using the golden ratio. We just know that it occurs. In plant life, the cells at the tip of stems are responsible for new growth. We call them "stem cells." Images of the stem of plants show small buds forming in the pattern of the Fibonacci series.[23] However, the reason why nature uses this pattern rather than some other spiral pattern remains a mystery.

The simulation of constant growth contrasted against the simulation of constant acceleration provides one explanation why Fibonacci numbers occur in nature. To be fair, it is not surprising that Fibonacci numbers occur in this particular simulation. The simulation assumptions require proportionality. However, this example suggests something far more complex. Rather than claim that growth occurs in two different systems following two separate sets of theories, I suggest that one theory governs growth in all systems: the Pull of Debt. A system following the constant growth rate of φ still feels the Pull of Debt. However, that system is constrained by proportionality. Both cases are the result of economic activity. Just as the Pull of Debt provides a reason why economic activity forms with constant acceleration, the same economic model of credit markets with constraints of proportionality provides a reason why growth might occur using Fibonacci numbers. The equations produce this result in simulations.

Fibonacci originally created this number series to explain a hypothetical scenario about rabbit breeding. In his scenario, a pair of rabbits produces a male/female pair of offspring. Every subsequent period the rabbits reproduce and no rabbits ever die. The Fibonacci series would provide the rate of population growth for any period. This is obviously unrelated to how populations actually grow, but it does relate to growth in markets under certain constraints.

To clarify one point, I am not implying that you can find the Fibonacci series in the stock market. There are many claims suggesting this is a possible way to make money. I am advocating that you cannot find the Fibonacci series in human economic growth, because there are not the same constraints on human's use of assets. There are also many examples in nature where growth occurs in spirals that do not use the golden ratio. However, I am advocating that you can create a simulation of a credit market that grows at exactly the golden ratio under a certain set of constraints. This simulation produces the same patterns that we often see in nature.

Another well-documented example of the Fibonacci series in nature is honey bees. A honey bee hive provides a more direct example of a credit market at work in nature. A hive has developed a very distinctive hierarchy, with one special female called the queen who lays eggs. There are many worker bees that are female, but do not lay eggs. The queen only keeps a small group of males in the hive for sexual reasons; they do no work other than to fertilize the queen's eggs. Females can become queens by eating a special substance called royal jelly. Once queens, they can leave to form a new nest. A beehive is the ideal example of a constrained and ordered system.

In order to maintain this strict social order, all male honey bees only have one biological parent. They are born from an unfertilized egg from the mother. Female honey bees require both a mother and a father. The impact from this reproduction method is that the family tree of honey bees occurs in the Fibonacci series (**Figure 32**). In other words, each generation will be the golden ratio of the previous generation as shown in the family tree below.[24]

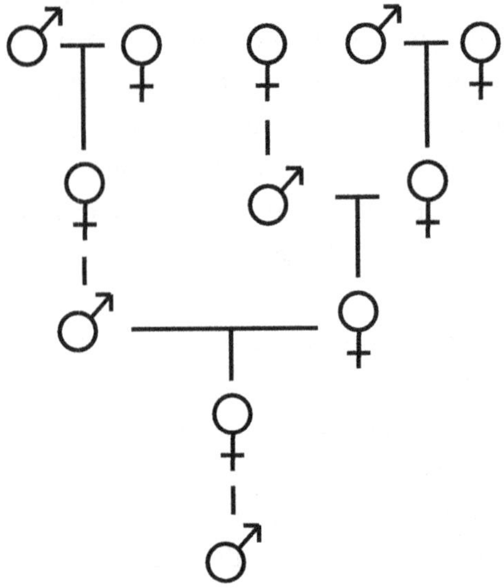

Figure 32. The family tree of a Honey Bee.

We can consider the roles in this society in the context of productivity.

1. the queen is an area of high productivity responsible for the production rate
2. the female worker bees are the assets used in generating production
3. the male drone bees are the assets engaged in reproduction

In this way, evolution has developed the roles of honey bees to conform to the model of credit markets. The hive operates under a number of constraints related to supporting the community. Females produce assets, and males are the means of changing the production rate (producing new offspring). The queen uses these roles to adjust assets and production resulting in growth under the constraints of the hive. The roles of the hive illustrate the two main drivers of the market: assets and production.

The reason why I am using these examples from nature is to show that growth happens both in economics and in biology, and the two relate through the concept of credit markets. What I am proposing is that these equations are not just useful to describe human economies. These equations describe the natural process of growth in life itself. The implications are immense. We as humans are so egotistical, especially business executives who assume that all economic activity is under their complete control. However, consider the possibility that natural laws drive economic activity, just like everything else in the world. In this way, economics is just an extension of the patterns of growth that occur in life.

To illustrate this idea further, consider another example from biology that is more familiar, the human body. Even here we see a pattern of exponential growth commonly referred to as the teenage "growth spurt." **Figure 33** shows data compiled by the CDC of average US growth in boys over time in kilograms (girls show a similar pattern).[25] Human growth also conforms to the pattern of constant acceleration, as the growth rate decreases over time (**Figure 34**). Of all the ways for the human body to develop, it is curious that it should grow faster and faster every year, resulting in a growth spurt as a teenager. However, that is precisely the pattern one would expect if the cells of the body operate under the Pull of Debt.

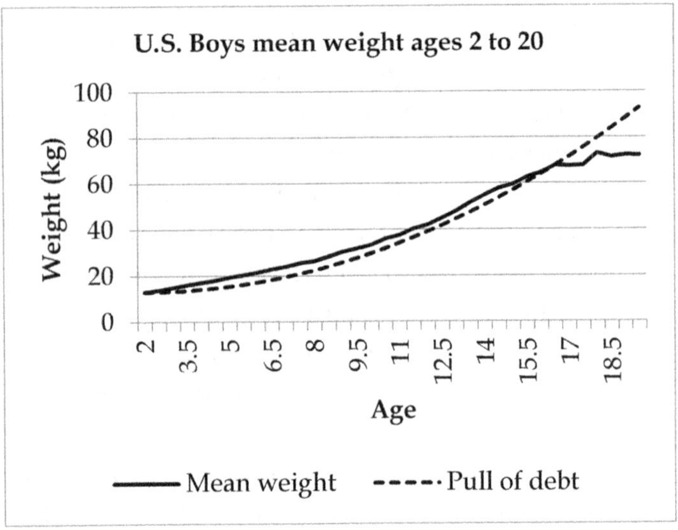

Figure 33. U.S. human growth statistics. Data from U.S. Dept. of Health and Human Services.

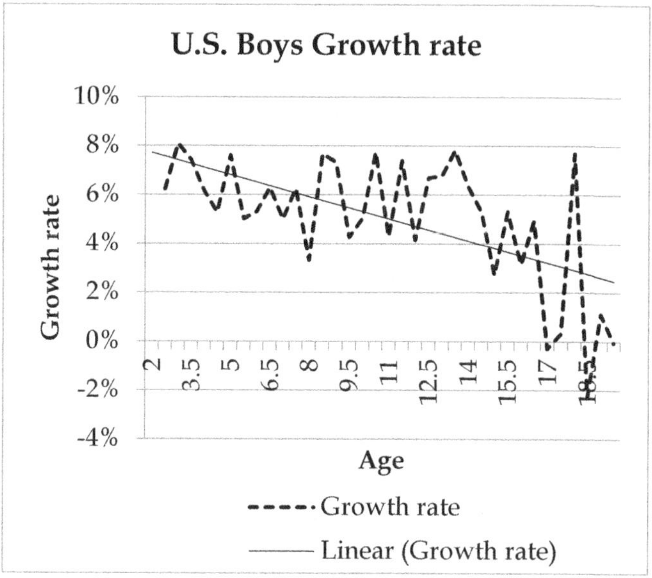

Figure 34. U.S. human percentage growth rates. Data from U.S. Dept. of Health and Human Services.

Interpreting this data, the cells in the human body are functioning like a credit market. They are engaging in debt arrangements that lead to growth using constant acceleration. The growth stops, when the entity reaches childbearing age, but continues in the offspring. Growth in the human body mirrors growth in society that also experiences constant acceleration.

Sex and business

I have suggested that we can find economic patterns in biological phenomenon as well as human interactions. If this is true, is there a difference between credit markets found in humanity and those found in nature? I would answer there is a difference. Humans have the unique ability to process abstractions. At some point in human history, human societies developed the concept of numbers. A number is an abstract idea that allows us to count things. The field of accounting is what separates man from nature.

Remember the example of a primitive human village in Part I. There is no money and no bartering, but the community interacts and forms a credit market. Villager *x* gives villager *y* food upon request. What makes this interaction possible is that villager *x* records a mental IOU. Villager *x* gives freely because reciprocity is expected later. If the roles reverse and villager *x* wants to use villager *y*'s spear, the spear is given and villager *x* adjusts the IOU. In this way, everyone owes everyone else and economic activity occurs within the market. Money is not important accept as a way to represent the underlying debt arrangements of the credit market. The ability to record debts enables humanity to unlock the power of credit markets in a way unlike the rest of nature.

Eventually humans developed accounting to record debits and credits in a systemic way. Luca Pacioli was a mathematician who lived in Italy during the Renaissance. Among his many accomplishments, he taught math to

Leonardo Da Vinci. Luca Pacioli wrote the first text standardizing the double entry bookkeeping method used among traders. This is essentially the same method we still use today and Luca Pacioli became known as the "father of accounting."[26] Accounting is such an important discovery because it made possible the human ability to place value on ideas rather than physical commodities that could spoil. Accounting allows us to place a value on intangibles like property, a patent, or a series of future cash flows. Individuals can rely on these values to form debt arrangements, because accounting records values in a systematic and reliable way. Accounting overcame our biological constraints and unlocked humanity's potential.

In a comparison of a credit market under constraints with an unconstrained system based on ideas, the most notable difference relates to sex. In an economic system that is heavily reliant on procreation, sex is a means for economic growth. Children are the work force of the future. If there is limited ability to develop new technology, having sex is a way to satisfy the pull of debt. However, the more individuals rely on intelligence, the less important childbearing becomes as an economic function. Humanity now has the option to grow by developing technology rather than creating offspring, and R&D investment replaces childbirth. Some people might consider it undignified that I am comparing sexual relations to an economic transaction. However, I am trying to provide insight into economic forces, and procreation is a factor in economic decisions. We see this effect in decreasing birth rates as countries become wealthier.

Accounting explains humanity's success in dominating the planet, but it does not undermine the model of credit markets for other areas of nature. Intelligence is not required for the model of credit markets to represent growth in a system. The pull of debt shows that societies will develop along a curve of constant acceleration, whether they choose to or not. Entities performing above or below the curve will not be as productive as those performing at the curve. Everyone else not on the curve eventually becomes obsolete, without any economic decision making required. Decision-making is a piece of technology that enables human credit markets to out-perform the credit markets of amoebas. However, decision-making is not necessary.

This is a significant difference from what economists teach in textbooks. Every economic theory starts with the concept of "rational choice theory:" that humans are rational players seeking to provide themselves with the greatest amount of utility.[27] This is the wrong place to start. Credit markets will form regardless of rational choices.

Consider the dawn of life itself. Imagine a pool of single celled organisms. Each cell exists on its own and grows by duplicating itself. Each cell probably has a different rate of duplication, some grow faster or slower than others. At some point, two cells happen to work together. The cell with the faster rate will produce and the second cell will use its resources to support the growth cell. We now have a multi-cell organism. This pair will quickly outperform the rest of the pool of cells. In an evolutionary system, the more productive organism will thrive. This is the same example of high and low productivity discussed in Part I, but the cells did not make a rational choice. Rather, they followed the path of least resistance to form a credit market.

Over time, evolution continued to develop credit markets. From amoebas to humanity, the same economic forces are at work. Markets tend to follow the pull of debt because it generates incremental amounts of insurance resulting in the highest productivity. Organisms that do not follow the pull of debt will either perish from fluctuations in the environment, or over-produce creating waste. Evolution will select systems with the highest productivity to continue developing life.

Markets without rational thought seem like a bizarre concept, because it is so different from our own experience of making economic choices. However, I argue the ability to make a choice is really a piece of technology that life has developed over a Billion years to continue along the growth curve of ever-increasing levels of production. Even today, I propose that evolution continues to influence humanity's growth by selecting areas of high productivity.

When I refer to evolution in this book, I am using the term in a much broader context than normal. We are used to the definition of biological evolution, but evolution takes place in economies as well. I am referring to the evolution of ideas. In a business environment with many different choices, the most productive choice will dominate over time. It is the same concept as biological evolution and computer simulations model it in the same way. People often describe Charles Darwin's theory of evolution with the phrase "survival of the fittest." If Darwin had been a businessperson, he would have used the phrase "survival of the highest ROA (Return on Assets)."

Eternal life

When humanity developed intelligence, it forever separated man from nature in the ability to harness credit markets. The Judeo-Christian story of Adam and Eve in the Garden of Eden is a fitting description of the birth of civilization. Adam and Eve eat the fruit from the Tree of Knowledge and God banishes them from the Garden of Eden. In this same way, humans developed intelligent thought. This ability allowed humans to harness the power of credit markets and bring humanity out of the jungles. Intelligence forever separates humanity from the rest of nature and human societies developed to rule the planet.

From the birth of humanity to the present day, civilization has experienced exponential growth. However, is continued exponential growth sustainable? Can economies really continue to grow exponentially forever? The interesting feature of the Pull of Debt is that exponential growth does become sustainable. Since the growth rate becomes slower as the organization becomes larger, growth is still able to occur forever without reaching infinity.

The Pull of Debt suggests continued growth is sustainable even to the point of creating eternal life. One of the possible scenarios science fiction writers have proposed for immortality is the transfer of an individual's consciousness into computer code and then transferring it into a robotic body. Under this scenario, the individual can live forever. What many people do not realize, is that this process has already occurred. Through the brilliance of lawyers, we have developed a legal entity called a "corporation." Corporations in the legal sense are people that can exist forever. They are formed from the ideas and principals of their founders. In addition, corporations are becoming more and more automated by robots. Eventually, humanity will completely transform into businesses, robotically run, and lasting forever. There is no longer a need for the human body. We have made the evolutionary leap from Homo sapiens to Corporations.

PART III: THE THEORY OF CREDIT MARKETS

Free will and fate

There is one more concept necessary to understand the Theory of Credit Markets: the variable for the fertility of the system (*F*). Part II discussed variable *F* in the context of constant acceleration describing the Pull of Debt (**Figure 35**), and all the examples held *F* constant at $1. However, *F* is perhaps the most significant driver in the equation. The relationship between the variables *F* and N^2 produces the distinctive curve of exponential growth we see in growth patterns. Understanding the variable *F* provides the key to unlocking the reason behind market movements.

$$y_1 = y_0 + \frac{1}{2}FN^2$$

$$y_1 = ending\ amount;\ y_0 = starting\ amount;$$
$$F = level\ of\ fertility;\ N = number\ of\ periods$$

Figure 35. Equation for constant acceleration in economic activity.

F defines the amount of constant acceleration. In other words, production accelerates by the unit *F* each period. N^2 creates the shape of exponential growth, but the curve accelerates or decelerates by the variable *F* in an amount that reflects the communities' productivity. In this way, we see that *F* is describing the relationship between the primary economic drivers: production and assets. This becomes the driver for a market's ROA. Things will always grow at different rates. Certain people grow faster or slower than others. Countries also develop at different rates. However, even though everything is growing at different rates, this one formula can describe the different growth patterns using the same framework by changing the value for *F*. This common framework becomes useful for understanding market dynamics.

Visualization can help to understand this equation. Consider dropping an object from the top of a building. That object will fall towards the ground with constant acceleration according to the Earth's gravitational constant (9.8 m/s^2). Now imagine you had a dial that would turn up or down the Earth's gravitational pull. Any dropped object would accelerate faster or slower depending on the new gravitational constant. The variable *F* creates this effect. Different countries grow at different rates, and they all have a different value for the variable *F*, which translates into faster or slower growth. This might be a difficult comparison to visualize because our experience with gravity always remains constant. However, imagine traveling on a rocket ship through space. As the rocket passes by different planets of different sizes, the different gravitational forces will affect the ship's acceleration. Different countries create the same effect with their different economic forces. This equation describes each country as if it were its own separate planet, each with its own gravitational constant.

This equation is a representation of a simple concept, that environments affect growth rates. The reason that different countries have different values for *F* is that they contain different levels of fertility in their environment. A country with a more fertile environment grows with faster acceleration and a higher value of *F*. Another helpful example is to consider a flower. In general, the genes in each species of flower instruct the plant to grow at some specific growth rate. Imagine a farmer plants two different seeds of that flower. The farmer plants one seed in fertile soil and the other in stony ground. Even though each seed contains the same genetic information, the flower planted in the fertile soil will grow faster than the flower planted in stony ground. Both plants start from the same amount of assets, but the plant in fertile soil has a higher amount of production from the same level of assets. Both plants still grow exponentially, but the plant in stony ground will grow much slower, because it takes more effort to produce the same amount of growth as the plant in fertile soil.

Unlike in physics, where constant acceleration functions in the equation as a constant, in an economic context the variable constantly changes, which makes the equation significantly more complex. The variable *F* changes over time as environments become more or less fertile. However, the degree of change is minimal because economic environments are usually slow to change. For instance, some of the factors that determine the level of fertility of an economy include laws, social behavior, political structure, demographics, and geography. These factors sometimes take generations to make significant changes. This equation describes the impact of environmental factors in their current state. Of course, events like natural disasters (earthquakes, meteors, locusts, etc.) can affect an organization's *F* immediately, but disasters by their very definition are rare.

From a human perspective, *F* really stands for choice. In the flower example, the farmer has a choice of where to plant the seeds. The "choice" between fertile soil and stony ground affects the growth rate. However, it is only a partial factor. The actual growth rate is partly determined by the exponential growth from the variable N^2 (which the farmer has no control over), and partly determined by his choice of F (which the farmer does have control over). In this sense, life is part predestination and part free will as defined by this equation (**Figure 36**).

$$y_1 = y_0 + \frac{1}{2} F N^2$$

Free will **Fate**

Figure 36. Free will and fate as defined by the equation for economic growth.

Running with the wolves

All the elements discussed in the previous sections of this book come together to form **The Theory of Credit Markets**. The Theory of Credit Markets says that all economic activity is the result of two factors.

The Theory of Credit Markets

Economic activity is the result of two factors:

1. A specific type of exponential growth (growth rates decrease the larger an organization becomes)
2. The level of fertility of the system

This theory enables us to predict the level of production in a system for any period in the future. Consider two systems, where assets in both systems start at $1. In the system where *F* equals .01, the actual growth rate over ten periods is 50%. Each period the production level accelerates by .01. In the system with *F* of .05, the actual growth rate over ten periods is 250% (**Figure 37**). The fertility of a system can have a tremendous impact on performance.

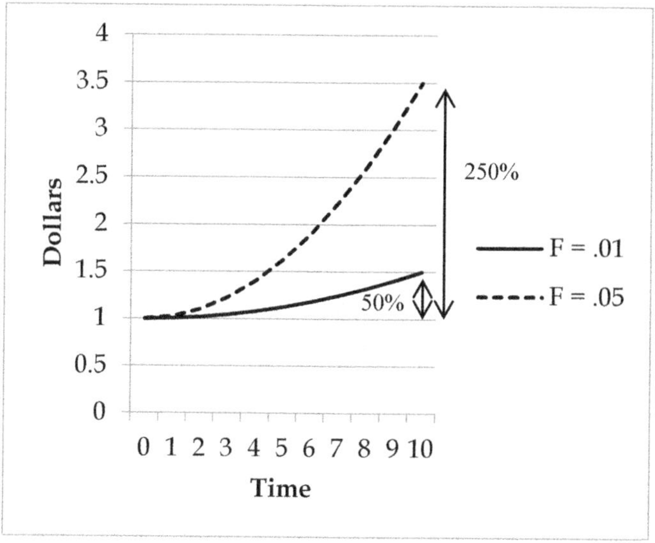

Figure 37. Comparison of different levels of fertility in the environment.

Another feature of the Theory of Credit Markets is that the concept is scalable. The theory works equally well to describe the dynamics between two individuals or two thousand. It all depends on how you define the market. For instance, individuals in the market have their own ROA, which interacts to produce the market's ROA. The market also functions as an individual and we can compare the market's ROA to comparison ROAs in other markets. This becomes endlessly complex because markets are not monolithic entities and sections within markets interact with other markets creating new entities. It is not practical to apply this formula to every single relationship within a social network. However, it is useful in understanding the underlying economic forces within a specifically defined situation.

The greatest downside to the Theory of Credit Markets is that in practical application it does not match the established accounting definition of assets. There is no way to look at an entity's balance sheet and calculate the variable F from an entity's ROA. The Theory of Credit Markets factors in economic assets used in production, like human capital, that traditional accounting ignores. Despite this incompatibility with traditional bookkeeping, the Theory of Credit Markets remains a powerful tool. This equation is useful for creating computer simulations of theoretical universes, creating long-term forecasts, and making investment decisions. It explains why capital will tend to flow toward areas with higher growth and therefore a higher ROA. Described another way, the equation explains that investors will invest funds in more fertile environments.

To recap, The Theory of Inequality explains how credit markets form. The relationship of production to assets defines an entity's productivity. Any group of individuals will self-select into areas of high and low productivity. The pull of debt explains that production levels will grow exponentially over time. This exponential growth takes the form of a decreasing growth rate as the size of an entity increases. The pull of debt occurs because it is the most efficient way to create systemic insurance in an uncertain environment. The Theory of Credit Markets explains that the level of fertility in a system increases or decreases the exponential growth of an entity.

To return to the example of the wolves described in Part I, we can see an example of all these concepts. The pack separates into areas of high and low productivity with the selection of an alpha dog. The pack lives together as a social unit, participating in a credit market. Individual members feel the pull of debt because of the need for insurance from living in an uncertain environment. Wolves advance their skills in hunting, fighting, and finding a mate. The speed at which this pack develops will depend on the fertility of their environment. The technology and skills of the group, as well as the environmental conditions affect the return they will receive from the pack's assets. Moving the pack to better hunting grounds will produce a higher return from available assets. One day the alpha dog will grow old and a younger wolf with a higher production rate will take his place. In this way, the roles of high and low productivity switch but growth as a credit market continues to march forward.

The point of this illustration is that economic development fits the framework of the Theory of Credit Markets. The theory describes a natural process that develops in all systems whenever communities form debt arrangements. Since this activity is a consistent natural process, we can define it through equations. The equations provide results that are useful to understand and predict the movement of markets. So the next time you hear a wolf howl at the moon, just realize that he might simply be trying to communicate his annual report.

Predicting the future

One of the greatest questions in Finance is "Can you beat the market?" What is ironic is the amount of disagreement between academia and Wall Street on the answer. Much academic literature starts from the assumption that markets are efficient and the market price at any given time represents all available information. This assumption implies that any attempt at investing in individual stock selections is useless. However, finance professionals make a living by claiming they can find inefficiencies in the market through undervalued securities. The real question at stake is whether it is possible to predict the future. Academia generally answers this question "no," while finance professionals answer "yes."

First, consider the case made by academia: markets are efficient and trading is useless. Probably the most influential academic achievement in finance is the Random Walk Hypothesis. This says that the motion of the stock market is random, and any price movement in a stock is equally likely to move up or down.[28] This concept suggests investment decisions are more a matter of probabilities, and that it is impossible to make decisions that outperform the market over time. A lot of superb academic work supports this idea. Bode, Kane and Marcus give one explanation in the scholarly text, Investments.

> Casual comparisons of the performance of the Wilshire 5000 index versus that of professionally managed mutual funds reveal disappointing results for active managers. The average return on diversified equity funds was below the return on the Wilshire index in 21 of the 37 years from 1971 to 2007. The average annual return on the index was 12.8%, which was 1% greater than that of the average mutual fund.[29]

In other words, the data shows that finance professionals actually perform worse than the market. The famous investing book, A Random Walk Down Wall Street, which also supports academia's view, explains "a blindfolded monkey throwing darts at the stock listings can select stocks with as much success as professional portfolio managers."[30] This idea has made "indexing" the popular current investment advice. If it is impossible to beat the market, it is better to invest in the market as a whole, or as diverse a portfolio as possible so it essentially mirrors the market.

The flaw in academia's reasoning is that over the long-term market movements are clearly not random. We know that the market has generally increased over time. If a system truly followed a random walk, this long-term increase in prices would never occur. A random walk would suggest that over the course of a century, the market should be at a net zero balance, or at least follow population growth. Yet market activity mirrors the economy and grows exponentially. Imagine if you lived at the time of cave men, and you had the opportunity to buy stock in "humanity." People would have certainly questioned your judgment, but in the end, it would have been a fantastically good purchase. The economic growth of humanity has not been a random walk; it has been a walk in one direction.

Now consider the case made by finance professionals. The most obvious argument is simply an economic one of supply and demand. If finance professionals could not predict the future, their clients would stop giving them their money, and they would go out of business. The mere fact that finance professionals exist, means they are providing some value. The second argument is that there are tantalizing examples of finance professionals making successful business investments over time, most notably Warren Buffet. The third reason is that market characteristics that traders learn by experience do not match academia's perfect description of markets: markets grow exponentially over time, and the best investments occur at the beginning of an entity's debt life cycle. These market characteristics contradict the Random Walk Hypothesis, which creates a dilemma. Either academia is wrong, or Wall Street professionals are wrong.

I propose that they are both right. There are two forces at work. In the short term, prices seem to follow bizarre, unpredictable patterns that support academia's Random Walk Hypothesis. Over the long term, prices follow the simple and beautiful curve predicted by the Theory of Credit Markets, which supports the position of Wall Street professionals.

Of course, predicting stock market movements is more difficult than predicting economic activity, because of the additional influence of supply and demand. The market price reflects both the fundamental value of the underlying entity as well as the supply and demand for that particular financial instrument. That is the reason stock prices do not always follow the same curve of the economic activity they represent. Sometimes market prices fluctuate extremely far from their underlying fundamental values: for example, when excessive demand creates a market bubble, or lack of confidence creates a market crash. Another example is a company buyback program that can inflate the value of a stock without any change in the underlying economic activity of the company. However, there is evidence that between the two factors determining stock price, fundamental value is more important than supply and demand over the long term. The text Valuation by Koller, Goedhart and

Wessels of McKinsey & Company describes a study comparing market prices and underlying company fundamentals. "The results show that the overall market tracks expected fundamental value closely over the past 40 years."[31] In other words, an accurate forecast of future economic growth would be useful to predict stock prices. Below is a chart of the S&P500 for the last 60 years (**Figure 38**). As you can see, there appears to be a resemblance to the same curve of US economic growth with additional variations caused by supply and demand.

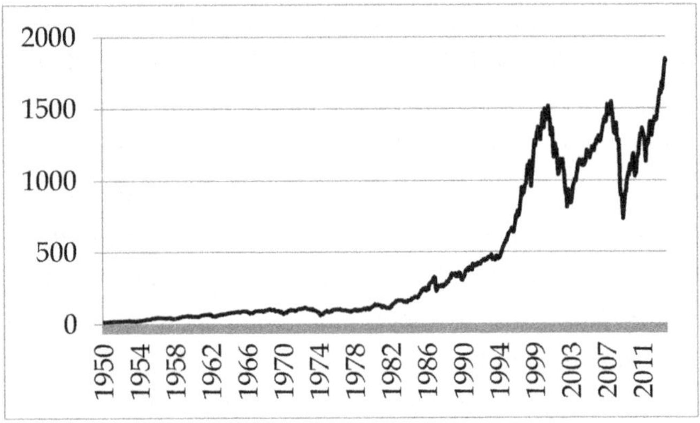

Figure 38. S&P 500. 1950 to 2014. Data from Yahoo! Finance.

Economy on overdrive

How does the knowledge of the new framework of the Theory of Credit Markets help you as an investor? The equations provide powerful tools to understand how economic forces work. You can apply the theory to economic data and reveal why people engage in trade, how to outperform competition, or why nations rise and fall. Business is ultimately about allocating resources. Business executives make choices about which opportunities will achieve the greatest benefit. When assets move to areas of high productivity, everyone benefits. This is the Theory of Credit Markets in action. The theory makes the additional connection that resource allocation leads to economic development through the pull of debt. The Theory of Credit Markets is the instruction manual for the engine that drives success.

The same concept of allocating resources is true for investing in the stock market. When people purchase a stock, they make a choice. The choice indicates that the people at a particular company can create a higher rate of return on that money than other alternatives. Let us not forget that a company's stock really represents the people who work in that company: the janitors, the workers on the manufacturing line, and the scientists in the R&D lab. When you purchase a company's stock, you are saying that those workers can be more productive with that money than you can. It is an area of low productivity transferring assets to an area of high productivity.

Investment books rarely discuss the role of investor as resource allocator. What they fail to explain is that investing is not about the stock market; it is about the "decision" to invest in the first place. Imagine you have $10,000. You have a number of choices of things you could do with your money. You could invest in home renovations, you could invest in education to increase future earnings, you could invest in a business venture, or you could purchase stock. Each of these options comes with some level of return. Your investment choice is a decision about which opportunity produces the highest level of productivity. Just like business decisions, investing is allocating resources.

Each investment is more than a transaction; it is fulfilling an important social function. Over the years, mathematicians and statisticians have dominated the world of finance with tools that analyze probabilities and price movements, sometimes without ever focusing on the underlying accounting documents. Our modern financial world creates further distractions with 24-hour news coverage and easy internet access to market data. It is easy to lose sight of market fundamentals. I am essentially arguing for the importance of fundamental company analysis. The finance professional fills an important role within society. These heroes of commerce glean information from accounting documents, identify the most productive companies, and ultimately produce the most benefit for society.

It is possible that our markets are not nearly as efficient as they could be. The philosophical clash between the ideas of efficient and inefficient markets suggests that more finance professionals are using index funds rather than fulfilling the role of allocating resources to the most productive. There is nothing wrong with index funds, but excessive index investing spreads capital evenly to everyone in the market, punishing the exceptional and rewarding the mediocre. However, imagine what would happen to the market if finance professionals spent more time targeting areas with the highest productivity and not funding the least productive. The more capital that flows to areas of high productivity, the faster the economy grows. This is the unique and special way that finance professionals can change the world.

A new model for entrepreneurship

The popularity of TV talent competitions, including business themed shows such as "The Apprentice" or "Shark Tank," has encouraged a misguided idea of entrepreneurship. These shows feature individuals who have some skill or idea. A panel of judges selects a contestant to give rewards and large amounts of money. While entertaining, I suggest this process is not representative of business in the real world. Those involved in entrepreneurship know that no one is going to "give" you anything; you have to make it happen.

Entrepreneurs build great businesses through hard work and determination. In contrast, people, who wait around for opportunities or investors, usually never get their businesses off the ground.

The Theory of Credit Markets provides a useful model for understanding how successful entrepreneurship works: an entrepreneur is someone who can control credit markets. We see this in numerous examples of successful entrepreneurs from Henry Ford (Ford Motor Company), to Sam Walton (Walmart), to Steve Jobs (Apple). Each of these giants of industry was exceptional at connecting areas of high and low productivity, and making a profit in the process.

If we analyze the entrepreneurship process, it reveals connections with the Theory of Credit Markets. Entrepreneurship starts with an idea, but a good idea is not enough. People have to buy your idea. The key is to connect your idea to some need or value creation for others. For the buy decision to happen in your favor, you need some sort of leverage or power over the other party. In economic terms, the entrepreneur achieves power through higher productivity. If you connect the idea to the customer's need through a clear value proposition, it makes mathematical sense for both parties to work together in some form of arrangement. However, that is not the end of the process. The entrepreneur then takes on credit arrangements himself. He figures out parts of his process he can outsource to areas of higher productivity. In this model, the entrepreneur is someone who can control credit markets (**Figure 39**). Profit is the difference between the nodes of the credit market: sales price to the customer and cost of employees to produce.

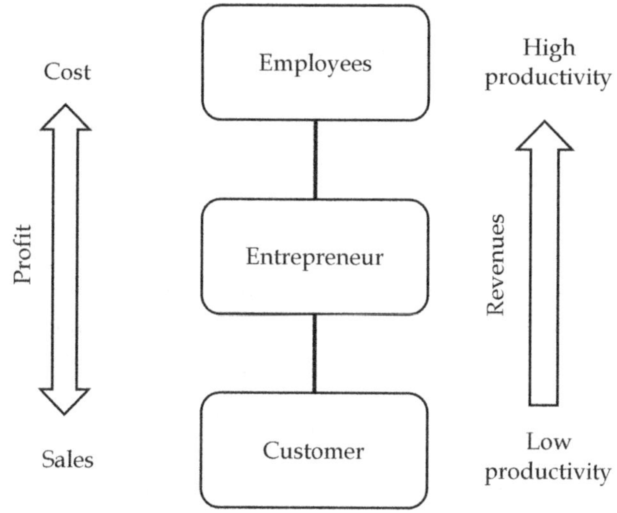

Figure 39. Model of Entrepreneurship.

As an example, imagine a computer programmer who wants to operate his own company one day. He writes the computer code for a useful program. This could be the most elegant computer code, but if it does not address a need, it will never sell. If the computer programmer can demonstrate to others how the program creates value for them, the product will sell. At this point, the program will need improvements to stay competitive, including software updates and customer support. The entrepreneur is most likely better off to outsource these duties to other people, rather than try to accomplish those tasks himself, so he hires employees. The revenue generated less the cost of the employee's time creates higher production than if the entrepreneur's time was used. The entrepreneur makes better use of his time navigating credit markets, creating connections between areas of low and high productivity in ways that make sense. This is essentially the story of Bill Gates and Microsoft.

The final step of the model is establishing the fertility of the system. Has the entrepreneur positioned the new company in a fertile external environment that is conducive to growth? Is the internal environment conducive to encourage continued improvements? Even if an idea generates revenue initially, a fertile system is necessary for long-term success.

Entrepreneurship is the most powerful form of investing: it is investing in yourself. Most people never realize that they are incredibly powerful. Every person has the entire world's credit market at their fingertips. It is a mindset. An entrepreneur sets a goal and then figures out how the current market can help achieve that goal. There may not be an immediate way to leverage a buy decision from a Fortune 500 customer, but there is someone somewhere who will realize value by forming a debt arrangement. This is the first step in a series of successive steps navigating credit markets to achieve your goals. If successful, entrepreneurs drive innovation for the overall market. Entrepreneurs provide new and better ways of doing things, and make all our lives easier. The Theory of Credit Markets is more than just an equation or theory. It is a road map for success and anyone can use it.

Moral absolutes

The concepts in this book present a harsh reality. Allocating resources only to the most productive in society can seem very Darwinian. My intention is only to explain that economies tend to favor those who produce, which can explain market movements. However, people should use caution before dictating social policy according to these equations. An extremist view would suggest that the sick, the weak, the elderly, the very young, and the poor should fend for themselves. The opposing view when tackling moral issues is reflected in the quote: "Every society is judged by how it treats its least fortunate amongst them." Churchill, Pope John Paul II, Dostoevsky, Truman, Gandhi and others have used this quote in various forms. I end this section with a warning to not apply The Theory of Credit Markets inappropriately as a means to achieve social ends.

PART IV: PRACTICAL APPLICATIONS

The Dividend Pricing Model

So far, this book has focused on theory, but there are also many practical applications of the Theory of Credit Markets. Current financial methods often do not place much emphasis on calculating growth. As a result, the growth factors used in many equations are loosely estimated and can provide misleading representations. The impact of these flaws goes unrealized by many analysts and affects decisions throughout the financial world. In contrast, the Theory of Credit Markets provides a more accurate representation of growth. These new equations provide more accurate forecasts and better guidance for business decisions.

Perhaps the most influential financial equation in use today is the Dividend Pricing Model. Most subsequent financial models use some version of the Dividend Pricing Model as the way to calculate growth. In 1959, Myron J. Gordon at the University of Toronto published the Dividend Pricing Model (also called the

Gordon Growth Model). Its original purpose was to value a series of reliable dividend payments, by calculating the present value of a series of cash flows (**Figure 40**). The model is useful because it produces a value analysts can compare against the current market price. The departure of the price from the underlying value creates a potential investment opportunity. The assumption is that sometime in the future, price and value will realign as the market realizes the discrepancy.[32]

$$P = \frac{D}{r - g}$$

$$P = price; D = Dividend; r = discount\ rate;$$
$$g = growth\ rate$$

Figure 40. Dividend Pricing Model.

The Dividend Pricing Model has been adapted for use in other areas of finance, most notably the Continuing Value Formula. In valuing a company, cash flows that are more than eight to ten years into the future are difficult to estimate with any measure of accuracy. Analysts use the Dividend Pricing Model as the Continuing Value Formula by replacing dividends with expected future cash flows. This determines a value for long-term forecasts. This approach has become quite common, and almost every company valuation method somehow relies on this equation. These valuations can effect stock prices, corporate take-overs, access to credit, and any number of financial transactions.[33]

The logic behind this method is that any company will find it difficult over extended periods to continue to grow faster than the economy. By using the US growth rate as the growth rate in the Continuing Value Formula, analysts value the long-term forecast as if the company grows at the same rate as the economy. This assumes the company's competitive advantage will erode over time. Historically, the US has grown between 4% and 8% per year. Analysts choose some value in that range to use as a constant growth rate. Even though the future cash flows are very uncertain, this method provides an easy way to calculate the value of the company.[34]

This common approach to valuation creates significant room for error. Apart from the arbitrary nature of choosing the constant for growth, analysts also do not take into account that the Dividend Pricing Model was intended as a shortcut. In 1959, there were no computers in common use, and calculating out complex forecasts was difficult. The Dividend Pricing Model provided an easy way to calculate increasing payments by assigning a constant growth rate (g). Keeping the growth rate constant, avoids having to calculate the present value of each payment individually. However, assigning a constant variable for g creates the following weaknesses.

1. The resulting value (*P*) is highly sensitive to the growth rate (*g*).
2. The growth rate (*g*) must always be lower than the cost of capital (*r*).
3. Using a constant growth rate does not always create the most realistic forecast.

Anyone using the model will encounter nonsense answers under any of these three conditions.

The reason the Dividend Pricing Model continues to be so popular is that these flaws have not really mattered. Since 1960, the majority of academic work focuses on the US stock market. One rarely encounters the three situations when valuing large-cap US stocks. Even if the value for the future growth rate of the economy is incorrect, as long as all the company valuations use the same faulty assumptions, the equation will still produce usable results. The comparisons will still show which companies are the most over or under valued. Since the Dividend Pricing Model is so easy to use, it has been the most cost-effective choice for valuations.

However, this method may no longer be a viable alternative. As modern financial portfolios become more complex and internationally diverse, it becomes more common to encounter the three situations where the model fails. Especially in emerging markets, all three conditions are usually occurring at the same time. First, different countries often have vastly different growth rates, which can skew the results because the equation is sensitive to the variable *g*. Next, the rapid grow rates in these economies are often higher than the cost of capital. Finally, it is a questionable assumption that these countries will experience a constant high growth rate forever.

The problem becomes even more significant when you realize the impact this small equation has on financial decisions. The text Valuation by Koller, Goedhart, and Wessels explains the impact of the continuing value equation.

> A thoughtful estimate of continuing value is essential to any valuation because continuing value often accounts for a large percentage of a company's total value. Comparing continuing value as a percentage of total value for companies in four industries, given an eight-year explicit forecast... continuing value accounts for 56 percent to 125 percent of total value.[35]

This text explains the impact this model has on final valuations. In determining the value of a company, the majority of the "price" comes from this small equation. This is troubling when we now operate in an environment where the Dividend Pricing Model fails on a more frequent basis. It is time to re-evaluate our approach to modeling growth.

Alternative approach using acceleration

The Theory of Credit Markets provides an alternative to the Dividend Pricing Model (**Figure 41**). Rather than holding growth as a constant, the Theory of Credit Markets uses a constant for acceleration (*F*). This produces a realistic forecast where the growth rate decreases each period (**Figure 42**). In contrast, the Dividend Pricing Model holds the growth rate constant and acceleration increases every period (**Figure 43**). The more complicated analysis of a changing growth rate may have been impossible without computers, but with today's spreadsheet applications, performing the calculations is easy.

$$y_N = \frac{1}{2}FN^2 + y_0$$

Figure 41. The Theory of Credit Markets

Period	0	1	2	3	4	5
Cash flow	100	105	110	115	120	125
Growth		0.05	0.0476	0.0454	0.0434	0.0416
Acceleration		5	5	5	5	5

Figure 42. Acceleration held constant

Period	0	1	2	3	4	5
Cash flow	100	105	110.25	115.76	121.55	127.63
Growth		0.05	0.05	0.05	0.05	0.05
Acceleration		5	5.25	5.5125	5.7881	6.0775

Figure 43. Growth rate held constant

Acceleration will also fulfill the same function by mirroring the growth of the economy or sector of the company being valued. Using simple statistical methods, the constant for acceleration (F) is determined from historical economic data. Then the equation from the Theory of Credit Markets will provide the forecast of production for any period in the future. The change in production levels determines the value of the growth rate (g) for each period.

Comparing the equations reveals the differences between the two methods. For a true comparison, it is necessary to use the extended version of the Dividend Pricing Model and discount each cash flow separately (**Figure 44**). This will avoid some of the flaws that appear when using the more popular shortcut approach. Each method will calculate cash flows out to 150 periods; after that point, the effect on present value is minimal because it is so far into the future.[36]

$$PV = \frac{FCF}{r-g} \approx \frac{FCF_1}{(1+r)} + \sum_{n=1}^{150} \frac{FCF_{N-1}(1+g)}{(1+r)^N}$$

Figure 44. Equation using the Dividend Pricing Model. G remains constant.

The Theory of Credit Markets allows the user to decrease the variable for growth each period. Using the typical equation to determine growth (**Figure 45**), the Theory of Credit Markets replaces the variable *g* (**Figure 46**) in the original Dividend Pricing Model (**Figure 44**). This method produces a present value using a more accurate description of growth.

$$Growth = \frac{Ending\ amount - Starting\ amount}{Starting\ amount}$$

Figure 45. Equation for Growth

$$PV \approx \frac{FCF_1}{(1+r)} + \sum_{n=1}^{150} \frac{FCF_{N-1}\left(1 + \left(\frac{\left(\frac{1}{2}FN^2 + P_0\right) - \left(\frac{1}{2}F(N-1)^2 + P_0\right)}{\left(\frac{1}{2}F(N-1)^2 + P_0\right)}\right)\right)}{(1+r)^N}$$

Figure 46. Equation using the Theory of Credit Markets. G decreases every period.

Charts can illustrate the differences between the two methods. **Figure 47** contains a chart displaying both the Dividend Pricing Model with a growth rate of 7%, and the Theory of Credit Markets using a value for *F* of 7.9. Both methods produce similar results over a 60-year period, which is remarkably close to the actual performance of US GDP.

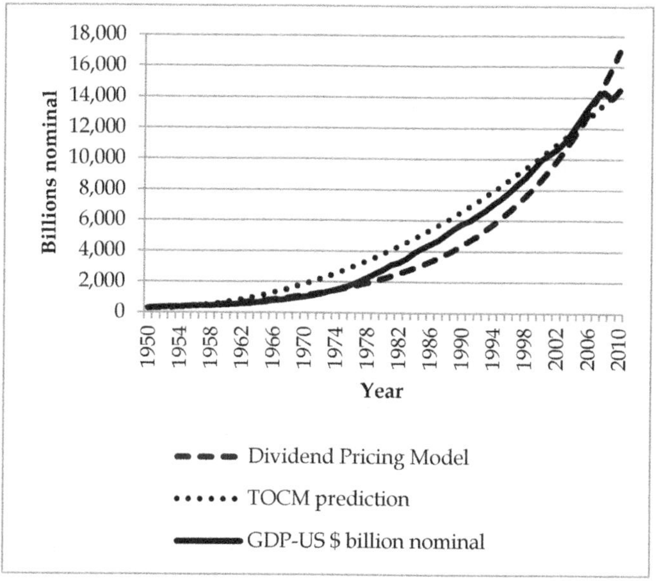

Figure 47. Comparison of forecasts using constant growth and constant acceleration.

However, extending the forecast out 150 years reveals how the two methods diverge (**Figure 48**). The Dividend Pricing Model grows rapidly in the future, dramatically outpacing the Theory of Credit Markets. Every time an analyst uses the Dividend Pricing Model, the model captures this unrealistic growth projection in the price.

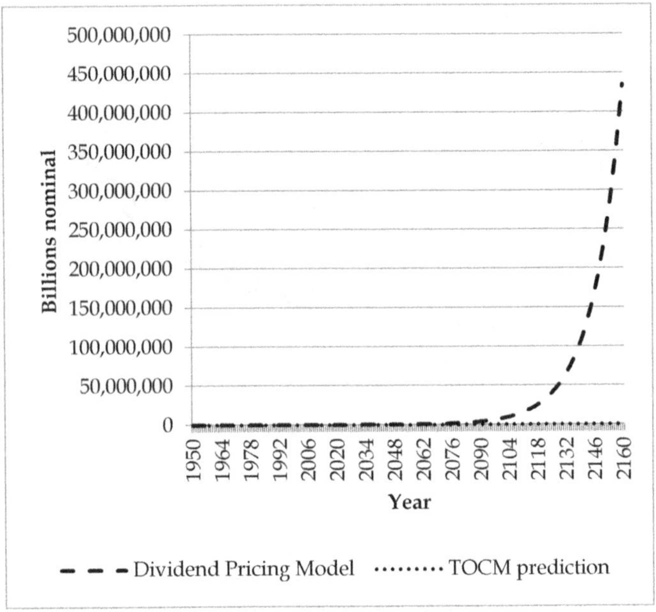

Figure 48. 150 year forecast comparing constant growth to constant acceleration.

In contrast, **Figure 49** displays a chart showing just the Theory of Credit Markets forecast against US GDP growth over the same 210-year period (including historical and future forecast). This provides a much more realistic projection of economic growth. These charts illustrate the impact these financial models have in valuation, as well as the benefit of using the Theory of Credit Markets to create a more accurate forecast.

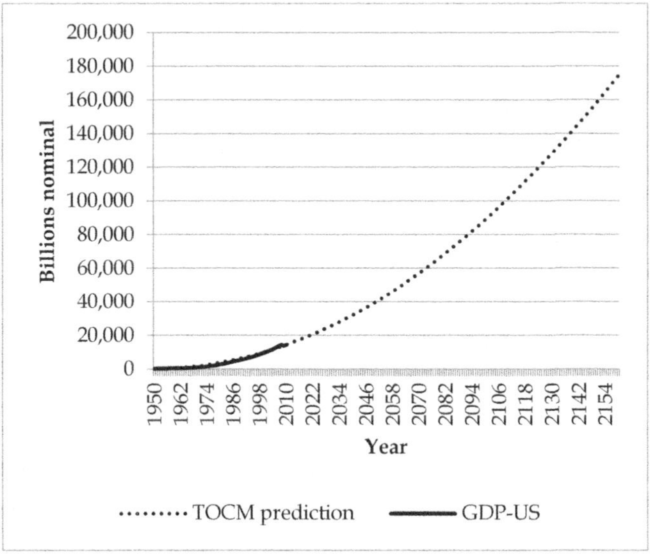

Figure 49. 150 year forecast using constant acceleration.

Weaknesses of using acceleration

Like any financial model, the Theory of Credit Markets has its own weaknesses. In fact, the Theory of Credit Markets may NOT be the most effective tool to make investment decisions. Understanding the shortfalls of any financial model is important in practical applications. Many other financial tools might be more appropriate. As mentioned earlier, the Dividend Pricing Model works for evaluating a specific type of portfolio: large-cap US Stocks. Understanding the weaknesses of the Theory of Credit Markets ensures that we apply the correct tool in the appropriate situation.

The first issue is the Theory of Credit Markets describes long-term market movements. It is best to interpret the results of the equations in decades. This obviously does not meet the needs of someone with an actively managed portfolio looking for returns every quarter. However, many organizations do make decisions that require long-term planning, and the Theory of Credit Markets may be the more appropriate tool.

The second issue is how to define cash flow. This book has previously suggested that businesses can use Net Income as cash flow in these equations. However, several other income numbers may provide better alternatives. It is debatable whether productivity calculations should emphasize Net Income over Gross Profit, since Net Income includes cash flows not associated with the core business. Other analysts might use EVA (Economic Value Added) rather than either income number. This book uses Net Income because it provides a concrete value for "production" of an entity as described in the theoretical model of a credit market discussed in Part I. However, the equations will still produce useful forecasts of growth, even when using other definitions for income.

The third issue is that not all growth is equal. Both the Dividend Pricing Model and the Theory of Credit Markets assumes all growth is valid. However, a company can grow for a number of reasons, which may not warrant the same valuations. Imagine two companies where sales have doubled. One company doubled sales because of an expanding market. The other company doubled sales because of a company merger. Obviously, the forecast for both companies would require different valuations. The Theory of Credit Markets does not automatically capture these differences and requires additional judgment.

Perhaps the greatest potential issue with the Theory of Credit Markets is the potential for error in determining the variable for acceleration (F). Acceleration is determined completely from statistical analysis of historical data. It is important that the resulting value represent a reasonable forecast for the future. As discussed in Part III, the equation makes a huge assumption that the level of fertility of the system will continue into the future. Often times this is reasonable because social change often happens over decades.

However, remember that people's choices determine acceleration. If people start making better choices, the fertility of the environment will increase and acceleration will also increase. If analysts expect the environment to become more or less fertile in the future, they should adjust acceleration (*F*), regardless of the historical data.

Additionally, the statistical process is highly dependent on the period the analyst selects. For instance, a country experiencing recent growth due to market reforms might have a more fertile environment than previous decades. If acceleration were determined by a more recent period, the constant would be much higher. Forecasted cash flows would be at a much higher value, producing a higher valuation. However, the uptrend could also be a market bubble, and the cash flows would return to previous levels and should be valued as such. Any statistical process involves a lot of judgment, and could become a source for error. However, when used properly, the Theory of Credit Markets can provide actionable information that was previously difficult to analyze.

New solutions for difficult problems

The ability to create a credible long-term forecast has many uses. It might seem that most business decisions deal with shorter periods. After all, how useful is it to know the production level in 150 years if everyone is dead by then? However, many of the financial decisions we make today depend on our understanding of future world developments. For instance, one major issue that affects many financial decisions is the relationship between the US and China. The Theory of Credit Markets can provide insight into the much sought after question: which country will dominate the world economy in 150 years, the US or China?

Questions regarding long-term forecasts are difficult to answer. Any review of economic reports on China produces a wide range of forecasts. Some analysts predict the US will dominate and some predict China. The conflict between these two views is the difference between the Dividend Pricing Model and the Theory of Credit Markets. A 150-year forecast created by both methods produces opposite results. With the method that uses a constant for acceleration (The Theory of Credit Markets), the US maintains the lead in total GDP over China (**Figure 50**). However, with the method that uses a constant for growth (Dividend Pricing Model), China GDP surpasses the size of the US in 2021 and continues to outpace the US (**Figure 51**).

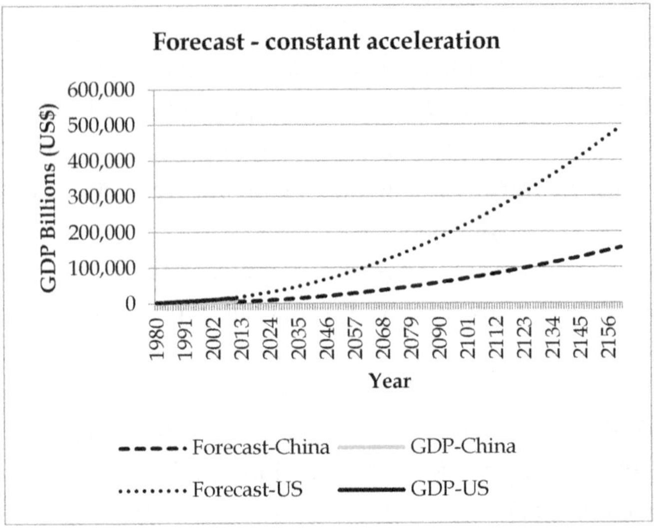

Figure 50. 150 year forecast for the US and China using constant acceleration.

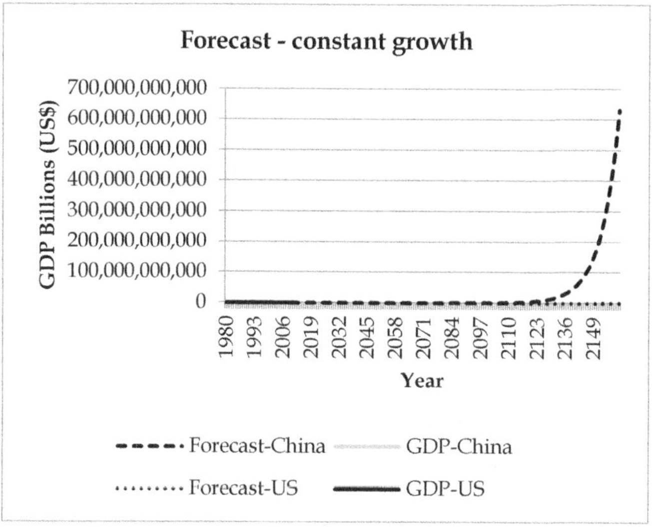

Figure 51. 150 year forecast for the US and China using constant growth.

These charts illustrate that someone's perspective on the future of world politics is dependent on their forecasting method. Many commentaries that support China's future dominance over the US assume a high growth rate will stay constant. China has a much larger labor force than the US, and continued growth does seem to suggest growing economic strength. Over the last 30 years, US GDP has increased by 420%, while China GDP has increased by 3031%. The alternative viewpoint would be to look at productivity. The production rate per asset is much higher in the US. The American worker is 11 times more productive than the Chinese worker is (although this gap shrinks every year). This suggests that even with a much smaller work force, the US GDP can continue to outperform China in the future. This focus on productivity is more in line with the Theory of Credit Markets forecast. After calculating the acceleration (*F*) during the last 30 years, the US is 26.0 and China is 12.8 indicating that business in the US operates within a more fertile environment. Moreover, in a simple visual comparison of the two charts, it appears that the forecast based on the Theory of Credit Markets appears to be more realistic.

The Theory of Credit Markets also provides the additional benefit of placing the US and China in a theoretical framework of a credit market described in Part I of this book. This framework helps to explain the market dynamics between the two nations. China holds a large amount of US debt. This fits the model, where China has low productivity and the US has high productivity. By acquiring US debt, China is actually transferring assets to an area of higher productivity in the US. The US agrees to share their wealth by transferring back the assets through regular interest payments to China. Since the US can utilize these funds (assets) at a higher productivity rate than China, both countries benefit.

This is an extreme oversimplification, but it illustrates an example of the gap between high and low productivity leading to the use of credit markets. The

Theory of Credit Markets helps investors to understand this relationship and make appropriate investment choices. Of course there is no guarantee that the productivity of nations will not change. As previously discussed in Part I, it is possible for the roles to switch through knowledge transfer and the nation of low productivity to surpass the nation of high productivity.

A new kind of ratio analysis

Another practical result of the Theory of Credit Markets is the creation of a new ratio. With a credible long-term forecast of 150 years, it is a simple calculation to determine present value. Comparing the total present value against the current stock price creates a ratio that functions much like a Price/Earnings (P/E) ratio. The ratio describes the amount of "total value" purchased by $1 of investment, or Value/Price (V/P) ratio (**Figure 52**). For instance, a V/P of $2 means that an investment of $1 buys the present value of $2 of future cash flows. A V/P of $1 means the investment is exactly equal to the value of future cash flows (something you generally would not want in an investment because it does not provide any margin for risk). An analyst could also construct a V/P ratio using the Dividend Pricing Model. However, as already discussed, the Dividend Pricing Model does not produce a realistic forecast. The resulting ratio would also be unrealistic and would not be useful for comparisons.

$$\frac{V}{P}$$

Figure 52. Total Value / Price ratio.

Analysts can apply the V/P ratio in much the same way as the P/E ratio, as a way to compare companies or sectors. The P/E ratio is perhaps the most commonly used financial tool because it is extremely easy to calculate. It compares the current stock price per share against earnings per share over the previous twelve months (**Figure 53**). Both ratios measure the difference between the stock price and the intrinsic value of a company's cash flows. The difference is that V/P measures the true value of future cash flows, whereas P/E measures historical cash flows, which can provide misleading information. The "forward P/E" attempts to correct this by calculating the next twelve months of cash flows, but this still only takes into account a small portion of potential future cash flows. The V/P ratio is more difficult to calculate than the P/E ratio, but provides more information.

$$\frac{P}{E}$$

Figure 53. Price / Earnings ratio.

V/P ratios have the same weaknesses as P/E ratios. Just like a P/E ratio, it would be misleading to compare ratios of companies in different industries or countries that operate in dramatically different environments. For instance, a company in the US will have a significantly different ratio than a company in Vietnam, because there is a different level of demand for the stock and the price includes a different risk premium. It is the most useful for comparing similar companies in similar industries. It is also useful to compare changing ratios over time for the same company. An increase in a company's V/P ratio usually indicates a drop in stock price if the forecast of cash flows remains stable.

V/P ratios can be useful in diversifying an international portfolio. For example, a simple BRIC analysis (Brazil, Russia, India, China) involves comparing V/P ratios of each country index. Using current earnings of the index as initial cash flow, statistical analysis can produce a forecast for the next 150 years. The analysis calculates cost of capital with the index beta, and uses the Theory of Credit Markets to discount cash flows and reach a present value. These four countries have similar economic development so deviations among the V/P ratios will reveal whether a market is over or under valued. Of course, this is not the only factor to consider in an investment decision, but it can provide powerful information.

These examples show how the Theory of Credit Markets can be a useful tool in financial analysis. The financial world often uses inaccurate descriptions of growth that affect valuations. The Theory of Credit Markets corrects the weaknesses of the Dividend Pricing Model with more accurate values for growth. It is fair to assume that any attempt to predict the future, contains room for error. However, a closer examination of these two methods clearly shows the benefits of forecasts produced with the Theory of Credit Markets. It fulfills the role of any good financial model, to provide information for better business decisions.

PART V: THE THEORY OF CONTINUITY

Defining economic truth

In research, truth is a relative concept. Whenever researchers think they have identified a universal truth, they eventually find a new realization that provides a more accurate truth. Research is a continual process to uncover better and more complete descriptions of the universe.

I argue that the Theory of Credit Markets is a positive step toward a better understanding of economic activity. A number of reasons support the theory's credibility. First, computer simulations based on these new equations produce realistic economic activity, while simulations based on traditional finance equations do not. Second, the equations make sense on a conceptual level and provide explanations for several unsolved business phenomenon. Finally, the equations produce tools that are useful for making better business decisions. All of these things provide evidence to support the

Theory of Credit Markets as a more accurate economic model.

Like any theory, aspects of the Theory of Credit Markets are difficult to validate as true. The equations are difficult to test simply because they deal with such long periods, on the scale of decades. It is impractical to make economic forecasts and then test the accuracy in 20 years. Additionally, there are too many moving variables. Unlike in physics where you can plug in constant values to solve for the remaining variable, in economic settings there are too many moving variables to reach a solution. For instance, suppose an analyst uses the Theory of Credit Markets to create a forecast. If the actual performance deviates from the forecast, the changing variable for the fertility of the environment can explain the delta.

The Theory of Credit Markets is not unlike any other financial theory. It has many useful applications, but also has limitations. As an example, consider the concept of a stock beta. There are multiple ways to calculate beta, and if you visit multiple financial websites, they will each report different values for beta for the same stock. Despite the disagreement around assumptions for the value of a stock's beta, beta is still a useful tool for making financial decisions, a tool people use every day. The Theory of Credit Markets presents similar value as a credible theoretical framework, and it allows us to begin to tackle the fundamental questions of how business works.

There is an even more compelling reason why the Theory of Credit Markets is true. It provides an explanation of economic activity based on concrete physical laws. This suggests that business is not merely a stand-alone discipline. Rather, the study of business intersects with the laws of biology and physics. I describe this connection with the **Theory of Continuity** that explains the fields of business, biology, and physics are all interrelated by the common constraint of the speed of light. The rest of this section explains the widespread implications of this statement.

The physics connection

There is an intriguing similarity between the Theory of Credit Markets and observations in the physical world. Part II of this book discussed the phenomenon that the larger an organization grows, the more difficult it is to continue to grow at the same rate. Part II also described the similarities of a ball bouncing against the force of gravity with the pattern of economic activity, because they both experience constant acceleration.[37] In fact, both phenomena use the exact same equation (**Figure 54, Figure 55**). This begs the question of how this equation explains both economic activity and gravitational forces.

$$y_1 = y_0 + \frac{1}{2}FN^2$$
$$y_1 = ending\ amount;\ y_0 = starting\ amount;$$
$$F = level\ of\ fertility; N = number\ of\ periods$$

Figure 54. Equation from the Theory of Credit Markets.

$$y(t) = y(0) + \frac{1}{2}Gt^2$$
$$y(t) = ending\ position;\ y(0) = starting\ position;$$
$$G = gravitational\ constant; t = seconds$$

Figure 55. Equation for the position of a falling object.

Since the effects of both economic activity and gravity are similar, it becomes possible to evaluate economic activity using equations from Einstein's Theory of Special Relativity **(Appendix 2 provides a brief summary of Special Relativity)**. Everyone is familiar with Einstein's famous equation shown below (**Figure 56**).[38]

$$E = mc^2$$
$$E = Energy; m = mass;$$
$$c = constant\ for\ the\ speed\ of\ light$$

Figure 56. Einstein's equation for Special Relativity.

Einstein's theories also agree with our notion of gravity from Newtonian physics. Newton's Law of Universal Gravitation explains that the force between two objects is directly proportional to the product of their masses and inversely proportional to the square of the distance between them.[39] The equation below (**Figure 57**) is how we understand constant acceleration in gravity. One of the definitions in physics is that $F=mg$. We can substitute in the equation to remove F and leave only the variables of mass, distance, and gravitational constant. Since mass and distance are commonly observable, we can calculate the gravitational constant with accurate and consistent results. When two objects move towards each other under their gravitational forces, they will accelerate using the constant rate of acceleration described with variable g.[40]

$$F = G\frac{m_1 m_2}{r^2}$$

$$F = force;\ m_1 = mass\ of\ object\ 1;$$
$$m_2 = mass\ of\ object\ 2;\ r = distance;$$
$$G = gravitational\ constant$$

Figure 57. Newton's Law of Universal Gravitation.

Newton's equations still hold true under Einstein's theory. The difference is that Newton kept space and time separate, whereas Einstein connected the concepts of space and time and suggested we exist in four dimensions in a continuum referred to as "space-time." This allows us to calculate how the warping of space-time corresponds to gravitational forces between objects of mass.[41]

Both Newton's and Einstein's approaches combine to provide our understanding of gravity. Physicists believe that space-time warps around an object of mass. The warping causes movement according to the Law of Universal Gravitation. For instance, the moon is orbiting around the Earth by traveling along the curvature in space-time created by the Earth's mass. Near the speed of light, the warping of space-time creates the additional effects defined by Einstein's equations. [42]

There is more in common between Einstein and Newton. The Theory of Special Relativity explains the following:

- The larger an object, the harder it is to move
- The faster an object goes, the heavier it gets
- The closer an object's speed comes to the speed of light, the slower time moves

These statements explain the warping of space-time that occurs near the speed of light. However, they are strikingly similar to the constant acceleration of gravity we experience on our scale. Constant acceleration means that the faster the speed of an object, the slower the rate of change in total distance traveled each period.

There are still aspects of gravity that are under debate, but I suspect that gravity occurs because it is the only way for objects to interact without violating the constraint of the speed of light. If acceleration occurred faster or slower, the equations would no longer work out. If acceleration occurs too fast, then objects would end up traveling faster than the speed of light, contradicting the laws of the universe. If gravity accelerated slower than constant acceleration, objects would slow down, never reach each other, and all motion in the universe would eventually cease. The warping of space-time occurs simply because it has to, in order to satisfy the constraint of the speed of light.

These equations work because measurements occur in different "frames of reference." To further illustrate this point, imagine a simple example of a rocket traveling at 100m/s with constant acceleration of $1m/s^2$ (m/s^2 is a unit of acceleration). The table below shows the acceleration (**Figure 58**). It may seem that this acceleration pattern would eventually exceed the speed of light. However, that is not what happens. Einstein predicted that as the speed of the rocket approaches the speed of light, time slows down. The occupants of the rocket would still think they are undergoing constant acceleration, but each period of a second takes longer to pass. In fact, the rocket could accelerate forever and never reach the speed of light. This is why physicists call the concept "relativity," because the measurement of the speed of the rocket is relative to one's frame of reference. The occupants of the rocket have one experience of their speed against time, while observers in a stationary position outside the rocket would have a different experience of the rocket's speed against time. In no frame of reference does an object travel at the speed of light.

Seconds	Speed
0	100m/s
1	101m/s
2	102m/s
3	103m/s
4	104m/s
5	105m/s

Figure 58. Table showing constant acceleration.

The question that Einstein should have asked was, "What happens if you start a business on a rocket ship traveling almost at the speed of light? And what happens if your supplier is operating a business on a rocket ship traveling at a slightly slower speed?" Businesses report financial statements on four periods in the year or quarters. As one rocket ship approaches the speed of light, the time between each quarter expands. Therefore, the quarters pass quicker on the rocket ship that is traveling slower. From their perspective, the business on the faster ship is generating less revenue per period than expected relative to their own periods. To use another example, imagine the supplier is attempting to get an invoice paid for the level of effort for the previous month. The supplier is moving on the slower rocket ship, but actually experiences a faster passage of time. The transfer of the invoice between the rockets is not going to reconcile with the observation of productivity, which is some rate over time. This might seem like an extreme example, but it illustrates how constant acceleration in economic activity coincides with the laws of physics.

Physics on Wall Street

The history of physics progressed from studies of large-scale phenomenon (the orbits of planets, gravity, and the speed of light) to studies on extremely small scales. Recent breakthroughs in physics focus on quantum mechanics (the study of behavior at the atomic level).[43] It is ironic that the use of physics on Wall Street has taken the opposite approach. The first notable use of physics to explain market data was a paper published by M.F.M Osborne in 1959 titled "Brownian Motion in the Stock Market."[44] Brownian motion was the phenomenon named after the Scottish botanist Robert Brown who first described the motion in 1826 by suspending pollen grains in water. The pollen grains would move in a random way, and Brown suggested the collision with water molecules causes the random movement. Osborne's paper suggested that the same equations used to explain random movements in particle theory could also explain the random movements in the stock market.[45]

Most of the academic work on financial markets since Osborne's paper has continued to be about random movements over short periods and understanding the "random walk" of the stock market. However, as this book has shown, over longer periods the random movements give rise to organization. This dichotomy is similar to the conflict in physics between Einstein's equations for large-scale motion and quantum mechanics at a small scale.[46]

It is interesting to consider why Wall Street experienced the opposite historical progression as physics. I suspect it is because in business, profit is the primary driver of research. A trader on Wall Street has to meet performance goals every quarter. An understanding of long-term market movements is not very helpful if a random movement in the near term wipes out a trader's capital. For this reason, I believe there is significant room for further study on long-term market movements.

Just as Brownian motion can describe the random movement of markets on a small scale, physical laws can describe market movements on large scales. We see the similarity by comparing the chart of an object in motion (**Figure 59**) with the charts of GDP growth of random countries displayed below (**Figure 60**). The Theory of

Credit Markets uses the fertility of the economic environment instead of the gravitational constant, and it fits historical performance very closely. If the charts of the individual countries are not convincing, the pattern becomes clearer in the chart showing the GDP of the world (**Figure 61**).

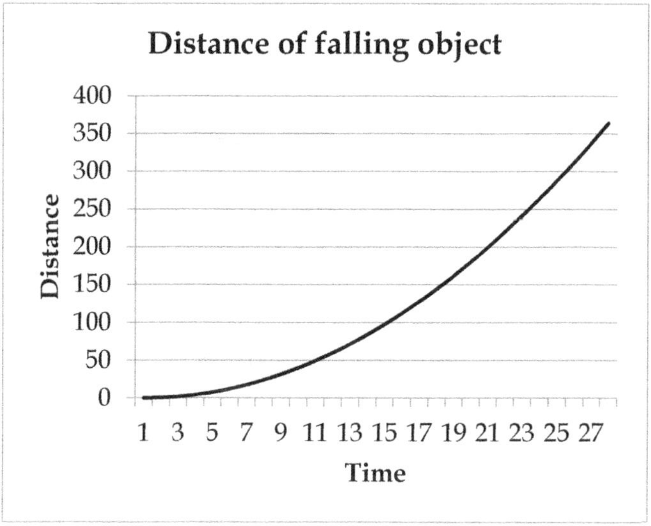

Figure 59. Graph of the distance of a falling object over time.

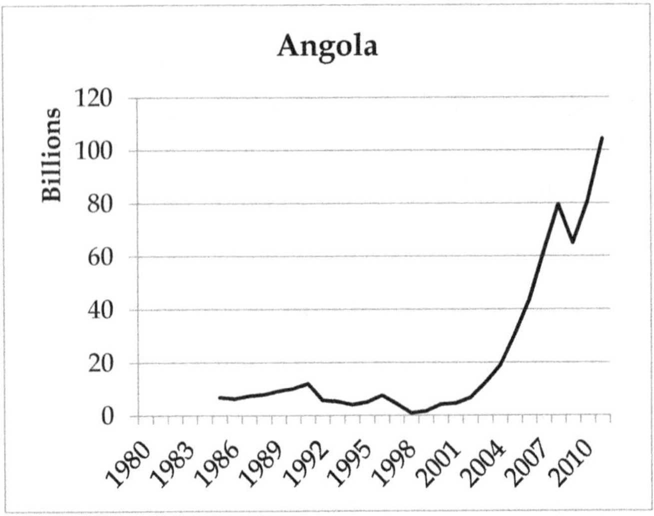
Angola
Billions
120
100
80
60
40
20
0
1980
1983
1986
1989
1992
1995
1998
2001
2004
2007
2010

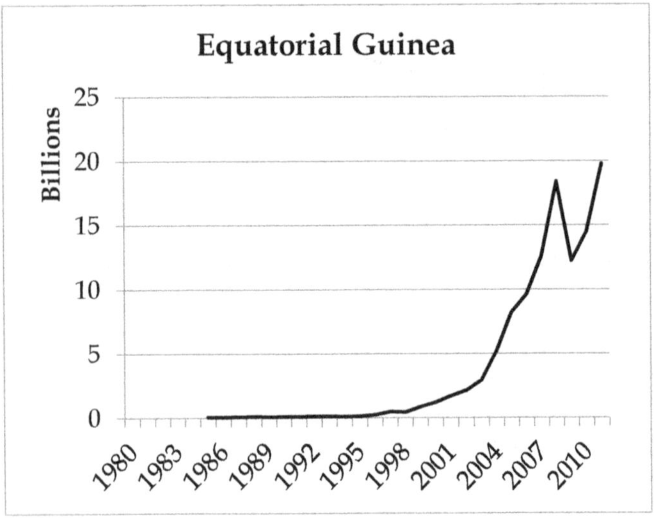
Equatorial Guinea
Billions
25
20
15
10
5
0
1980
1983
1986
1989
1992
1995
1998
2001
2004
2007
2010

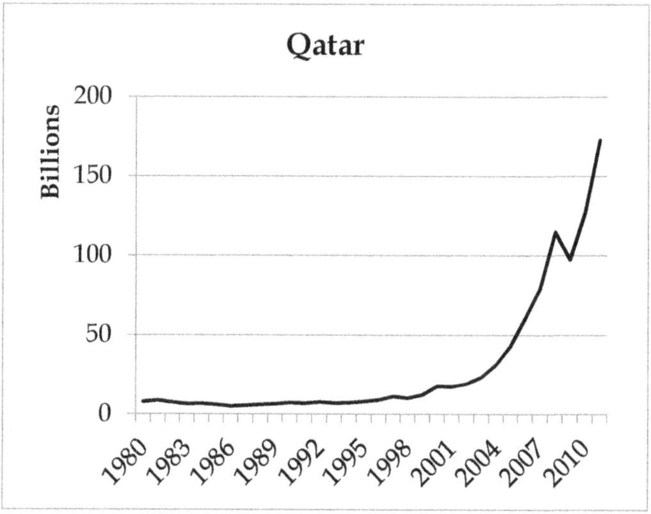
Qatar
Billions
200
150
100
50
0
1980
1983
1986
1989
1992
1995
1998
2001
2004
2007
2010

Kazakhstan
Billions
200
150
100
50
0
1980
1983
1986
1989
1992
1995
1998
2001
2004
2007
2010

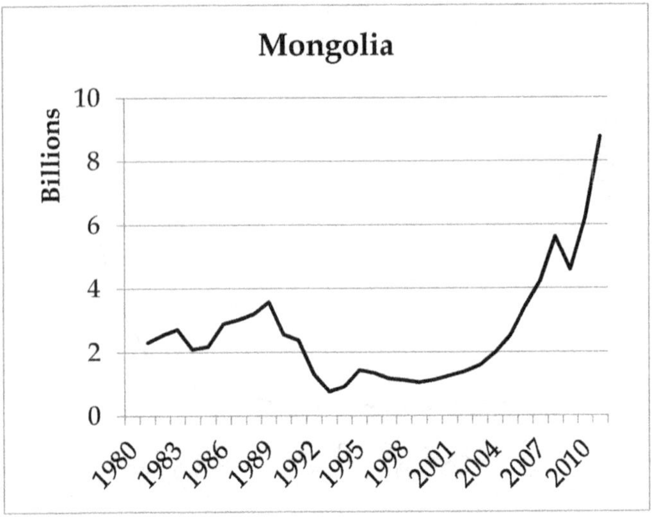
Mongolia
Billions
10
8
6
4
2
0
1980
1983
1986
1989
1992
1995
1998
2001
2004
2007
2010

Russian Federation
Billions
2,000
1,500
1,000
500
0
1980
1983
1986
1989
1992
1995
1998
2001
2004
2007
2010

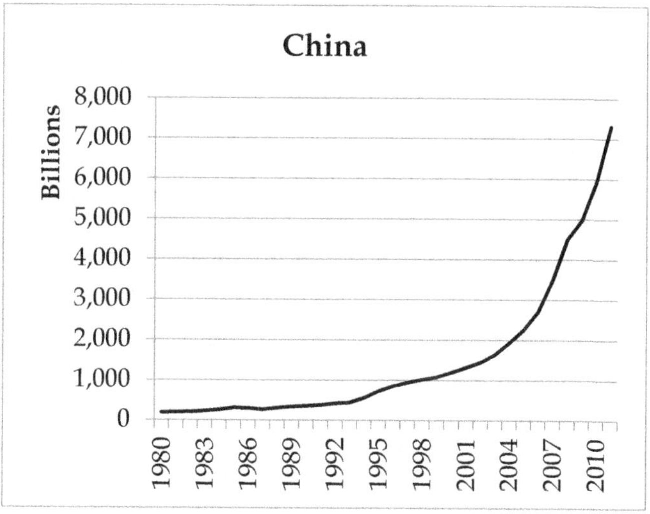
China
Billions
8,000
7,000
6,000
5,000
4,000
3,000
2,000
1,000
0
1980
1983
1986
1989
1992
1995
1998
2001
2004
2007
2010

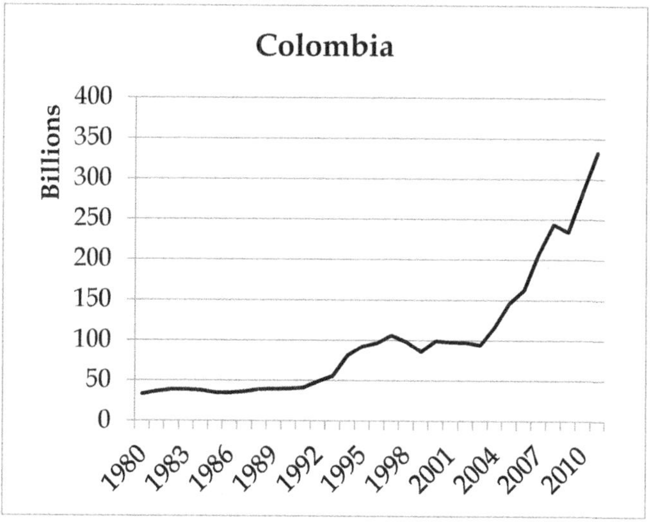
Colombia
Billions
400
350
300
250
200
150
100
50
0
1980
1983
1986
1989
1992
1995
1998
2001
2004
2007
2010

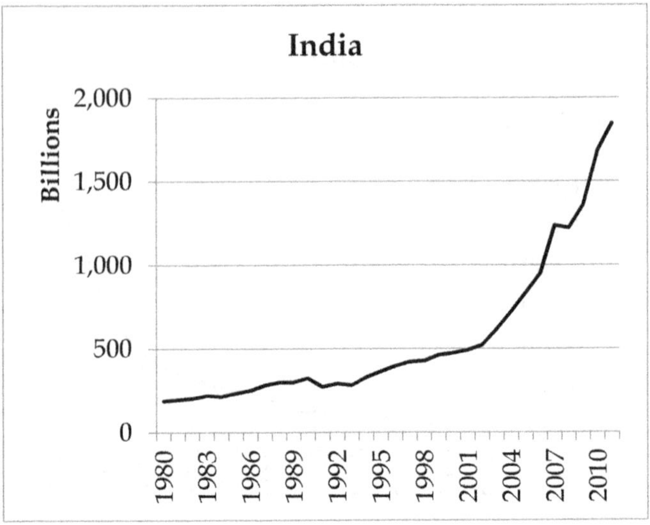
India
Billions
2,000
1,500
1,000
500
0
1980
1983
1986
1989
1992
1995
1998
2001
2004
2007
2010

Brazil
Billions
3,000
2,500
2,000
1,500
1,000
500
0
1980
1983
1986
1989
1992
1995
1998
2001
2004
2007
2010

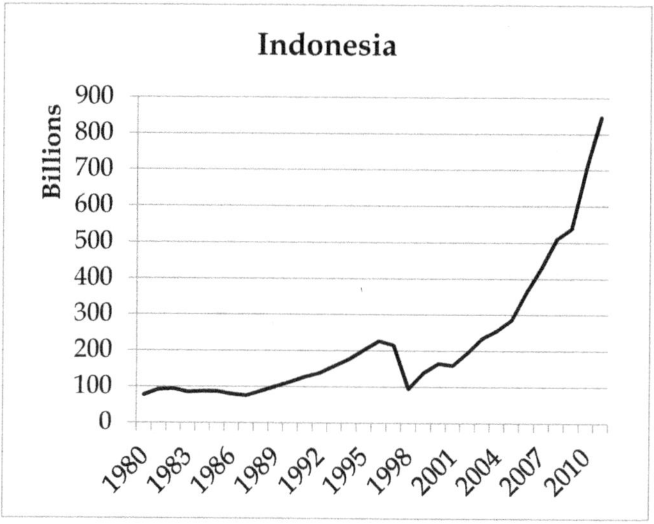

Figure 60. GDP by nation in current US$.[47]

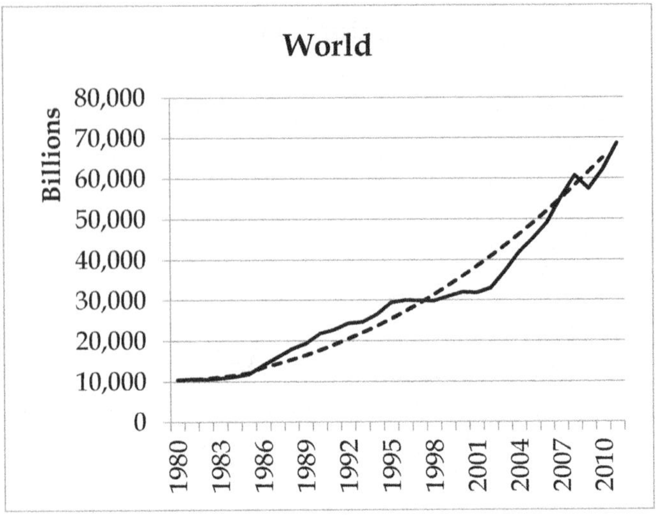

Figure 61. GDP of the world compared with the Theory of Credit Markets.[48]

For clarity, the Theory of Credit Markets does not suggest that everyone will experience growth. Clearly, some individuals and businesses will be failures. However, growth rates occur within some distribution and markets overall seem to experience growth. The US economy for instance contains many business failures as well as successes. However, as an economy, the US continues to experience growth.

The examples so far have shown that there is a similarity between physical laws and economic activity. This raises a question of whether the relationship goes beyond similarity and there is an actual connection. I propose that Einstein's theory does not go far enough. Extending Einstein's equations for Special Relativity reveals the connection between physics and business. *The speed of light does not only act as a constraint on objects in motion through space-time, but also constrains "processes" that occur across space-time.* I propose the same physical laws that dictate the motion of objects also influence processes. The universe is full of objects in motion, but those objects are also involved in processes. The problem is that the study of physics focuses primarily on objects in motion and may not have the vocabulary to properly define and analyze processes.

However, business has developed the exact tools needed to understand processes. The two main financial statements in accounting describe a process over a set time. The balance sheet provides a picture of assets at two points in time: the beginning and end of a period. The income statement provides production between those two points in time. These two documents create a description of a process using the two variables, production and assets, as described in Part I of this book. These two variables are the drivers behind all debt arrangements and the basis of economic activity. As discussed in Appendix 2, Einstein's Theory of Special Relativity can be described with a right triangle. Production and assets also happen to fit perfectly into the triangle used in Einstein's Theory of Special Relativity as shown below (**Figure 62**). The substitution of economic terms into the Theory of Special Relativity is the basis for the Theory of Continuity (**Figure 63**).

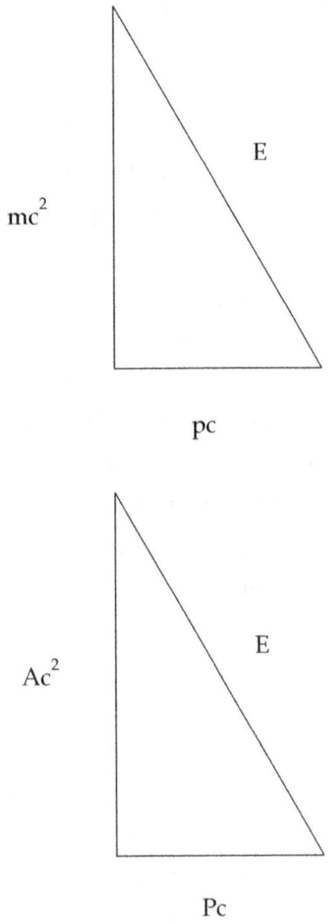

Figure 62. Triangles showing the similar relationship between physics and economic variables.

$$E^2 = (pc)^2 + (mc^2)^2$$
$$E = Energy;\ m = mass;\ p = momentum;$$
$$c = constant\ for\ the\ speed\ of\ light$$

Figure 63. Einstein's Theory of Special Relativity.

$$E^2 = (Pc)^2 + (Ac^2)^2$$

$$E = Energy;\ A = Assets;\ P = Production;$$
$$c = constant\ for\ the\ speed\ of\ light$$

Figure 64. Equation for the Theory of Continuity.

The Theory of Continuity

1. The fields of business, biology, and physics are all interrelated by the common constraint of the speed of light.
2. The speed of light does not only act as a constraint on objects in motion through space-time, but also constrains "processes" that occur across space-time.

The Theory of Continuity shows how assets and production relate to the speed of light, and how economic activity relates to the laws of physics. You can see how the size of the business (assets) and velocity of the business (production) fit the two sides of the triangle. The long side of the triangle, energy, limits both production and assets. Therefore, if a business has assets, there will never be enough energy in the universe for production to exceed the speed of light. This explains why economic activity displays the same constant acceleration as gravity and why we find similarities between business and physics. Both business processes and objects in motion are constrained by the same speed of light.

This suggests that the real equation behind Special Relativity is actually a business equation. The equation simplifies down to "energy equals assets times the speed of light squared." What this implies is that if you counted every single atom in a business, you could calculate the "rest energy" of the atoms that make up the assets. All the people, machines, buildings, and land contain the atomic energy of many nuclear bombs. The more practical application is to create a new definition of assets that aligns with the Theory of Continuity. Then it is theoretically possible to create an accounting system where the financial reports (**Figure 65**) track performance according to Einstein's triangle (**Figure 66**). We can then always calculate assets and income in relation to energy, which provides a unified method for tracking performance of processes across different frames of reference.

Balance Sheet

Assets = Liabilities + Owners Equity

Income Statement

Revenue - Expenses = Net Income

Figure 65. The equations of the two main financial statements.

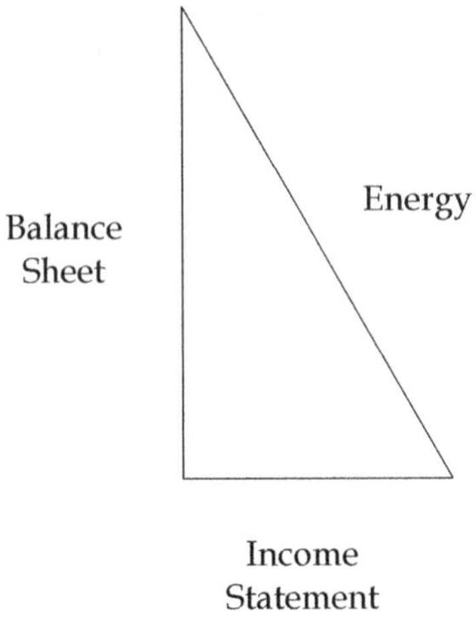

Figure 66. Diagram of an accounting system based on Einstein's triangle.

You might find such calculations currently unnecessary, but the practical applications are not far off. In the near future, humanity is going to be traveling in spacecraft exploring the solar system. I expect even sooner, that humanity will establish a colony and mining operations on the moon. There are many practical questions of how to set up such an operation.

Luckily, there is a historical precedent of an appropriate business model. In 1607, the first settlers arrived at Jamestown, the first permanent English settlement in the New World[49] (Roanoke was technically the first English settlement, but disappeared without a trace[50]). What many people forget is that Jamestown was a business. Jamestown started with investors forming a joint stock company called the Virginia Company of London. King James I of England provided a patent granting permission to explore the territory, but all the financial backing came from stockholders in the company.[51] Jamestown had its share of problems; many of the original settlers died and some even resorted to cannibalism.[52] However, Jamestown did eventually become a resounding success and laid the foundation for what would eventually become the United States of America.

If we follow the same successful business model to settle the moon, we run into a problem. The warping of space-time that is encountered during space travel makes creating accurate financial statements impossible. Any settlement on the moon will exist on a different spatial body from the businesses that are operating on the surface of the planet Earth. The same warping of space-time experienced on rocket ships traveling near the speed of light will also occur for businesses on the moon. Warping in space-time will cause individuals in different frames of reference to experience accounting quarters differently. GPS satellites solve the same problem with equations from Special Relativity. However, in this case stockholders on Wall Street need a common frame of reference in order to judge performance of a process, whether on the surface of Earth, on the moon, or traveling through space.

To use another example, imagine you owned a cleaning business that operated on spaceships traveling throughout the galaxy. Efficiency metrics for your employees are usually measured in square feet cleaned per hour. However, since each employee is traveling at a different speed in a different direction, each employee's measurement of a foot and an hour is different. Meanwhile an analyst is sitting behind a desk on Wall Street attempting to value your cleaning business, and needs to determine a single metric that describes the efficiency of the entire company in ft^2/hr. Current accounting systems provide inaccurate results under this scenario, because simply rolling up efficiency metrics does not take into account the warping of space and time. An accounting system based on the Theory of Continuity solves this problem. In fact, space travel requires the use of the Theory of Continuity in order to create financial statements that accurately measure processes. The benefit is that Wall Street is no longer contained to the surface of the planet Earth, but can become an organization that finances business operations throughout the universe.

The beginning of the universe

Consider an example of how the Theory of Continuity actually occurs. Physics tells us how objects in motion interact. How then does the universe develop processes? Imagine the state of objects at the beginning of the universe. There are two spheres floating in space. They could be anything: chemical compounds or asteroids. For the ease of imagination, just imagine two undefined spheres. Without any outside influence, the mass from these two spheres will interact in relation to the bending of space-time through the gravitational forces between them. The two spheres will be drawn together and collide. When the two objects interact with each other, there is likely to be some kind of energy transfer. Physics uses the Law of Conservation of Energy (which forms the basis for the First Law of Thermodynamics) to explain that the total energy of a system remains constant.[53] Since the event cannot create or destroy energy, it could turn into something else, like a chemical reaction between the two objects. We can describe this reaction as some level of productivity. The reaction will produce something from the assets of the system. The level of production will also depend on the environment. A fertile environment will create a more productive reaction and a hostile environment will create a less productive reaction.

It is my suggestion that these types of chemical reactions will follow similar patterns to those in gravity. For instance, consider the chemical reaction of fire. Fire consumes fuel and produces heat at different rates for different fuel sources. It will consume the fuel over some period in space-time. Because of the constraints of the speed of light, the process will occur with constant acceleration. This must be the case, because the process is occurring through space-time. If the reaction is too fast, it could exceed the speed of light, which would violate the laws of the universe. Too slow and the energy might not be used up in the reaction as required by the law of conservancy. It is reasonable to assume that other factors can also influence the rate of growth, just as gusts of wind can affect the pull of an object under the force of gravity. Additional constraints within the environment can influence growth patterns (such as the example of Fibonacci numbers in Part II). However, assuming there are no additional constraints, growth will tend to occur using constant acceleration. Another way to think about the process is that energy flows along the path of least resistance. Additionally, the fertility of the environment affects the rate of production by some variable. A fire will be more productive in a sunny environment than a rainy environment. The collision of two objects must create a process that follows this pattern so it does not violate the laws of the universe.

Now consider multiple processes occurring simultaneously within the context of a system. Over time, more spheres collide in space-time causing chemical reactions. Each pair of spheres is going to have a certain set of criteria based on mass, distance, and environmental conditions resulting in a slightly different reaction. Whenever you have a system of colliding spheres, it suddenly becomes an evolutionary system. The most productive reactions will occur more often and produce better results. Reactions on the fast and slow ends of the scale will waste resources. They will either burn out or not produce enough. The same concepts hold true as in biological evolution and the most productive reactions will be favored over time. It is as if the system tracks its productivity with financial statements according Einstein's triangle. The result is a system that develops in an organized way according to the Theory of Continuity.

It might be difficult to understand how random chemical reactions can display organization. However, by defining the boundaries of some environment, the conditions within that environment will inherently contain some optimal curve for chemical reactions. Of course, reactions do occur faster and slower than this curve, but result in lower productivity than reactions that occur along the curve. As a result, over extended periods the system will tend toward performance at the optimal curve.

This provides an explanation for the concept of "self-ordering" that often puzzles scientists. Some unanswered questions in science include, "Why does the universe appear to be self-ordering? In a supposed chaotic world, why do shapes take symmetrical forms? Why do distinct structures form in landscapes? Why do events occur in regular rhythms?" I suggest that self-ordering takes place based on the pattern of chemical reactions I have just described. This creates the beauty of the self-ordering universe we experience.

These concepts provide a framework for understanding the development of the universe since the dawn of time:

1. Individual chemical reactions occur.
2. Evolution selects the most productive reactions.
3. Productivity levels develop along a curve of constant acceleration adjusted for the fertility of the environment.
4. Complex organization eventually emerges.

One analogy that is helpful is to think of the universe as a giant blackjack game. There are a set number of elementary particles, much like a deck of cards. And similar to the randomness of a shuffled deck of cards, the particles interact randomly on a very small scale using Brownian motion. The interaction between the particles forms some level of productivity. And just like hands in blackjack, the combinations range from good to bad. However, once the cards are dealt, the rules change. The blackjack analogy no longer applies as natural laws begin to shape the previously random particles. Einstein famously said, "God does not play dice with the universe," comparing the randomness of quantum mechanics with the order of Special Relativity. The laws of space and time in our universe dictate that once the interaction occurs, processes must play out without violating the speed of light. At that point, Brownian motion gives way to the beautiful curve of development towards a self-organizing system. If progress did not follow that curve, the initial interaction could never have happened. The speed of light demands either an organized system, or nothingness. What we experience today is essentially a series of winning streaks in blackjack played out since the beginning of the universe.

Of course, this process remains a conceptual abstraction, because it is ambiguous as to how one defines productivity for a chemical reaction. Would it be relevant to measure energy used or mass created? In the origin of the universe, it is unclear as to the best way to measure productivity. However, after roughly 14 billion years, humanity has finally developed an objective way to measure productivity... money. Money is the market's way to value the productivity of a process. With 100 years of solid economic data, we can finally begin to see the beautiful curve of constant acceleration in the production levels of our processes.

From geology to biology

Part II discussed how single celled organisms could evolve into multi-celled organisms. However, that still leaves the question of how living cells developed in the first place. Living organisms, at their basic level, are nothing more than a series of chemical reactions. Since both a living cell and a rock surface undergo chemical reactions, scientists have searched for a way to draw a line that distinguishes the two. However, most attempts at defining "life" have met with difficulty, because the distinction is often a grey area. Different definitions of life vary, but generally include the following seven characteristics (**Figure 67**).[54]

1. Homeostasis: regulation of internal environment to maintain a constant state (ex. temperature)
2. Organization: structurally composed of cells
3. Metabolism: transformation of energy by converting chemicals into cellular components and decomposing organic matter
4. Growth: increases in size in all of its parts
5. Adaptation: ability to change over time in response to the environment
6. Response to stimuli
7. Reproduction: ability to produce new individual organisms

Figure 67. Seven characteristics of life.

I would like to offer a different interpretation of these characteristics. Life is a continuation of the overall process of self-organization of the universe. Chemical reactions will follow a development curve that will eventually produce the seven pieces of technology that we have come to recognize as life. I suspect that we will never find one "moment" when life appeared. It is more likely an ongoing process of chemical reactions organizing into forms with higher productivity.

In this interpretation, there is not that much difference between a rock and living cells. In fact, given enough time, a rock will eventually turn into life. A rock is a combination of elements. Certain conditions in the rock's environment, such as gravitational forces and the presence of energy, will determine the fertileness of the environment. Energy might come from the sun or running water. The influence of energy affecting the elements on the face of the rock will lead to some sort of chemical reaction. In an evolutionary structure, the more productive chemical reactions will become more prevalent. When two chemical reactions occur at the same time and benefit each other, a credit market forms. This chemical reaction will "grow" and quickly separate itself from the non-living chemical reactions.

For example, consider a living cell. It includes molecules performing different functions. Molecules specialize in different structures including the cell membrane, DNA, mitochondria, etc. All these structures work together supporting each other. It is like a credit market on a molecular level where the cell structures are engaged in business arrangements. Molecules that display this level of cooperation will experience more productive chemical reactions, then molecules that act alone. It is easy to see how life is a further development of previous chemical processes, and how evolution selects the more productive processes to form life.

The great realization of this concept is that life MUST occur. We were not some accident. Chemical reactions in the universe will always eventually develop into life as the process of self-ordering continues to higher levels of productivity. Of course, the speed at which this development occurs depends on the fertility of the environment. However, even in hostile environments, this concept implies that self-ordering towards life will still occur, just very slowly. I discussed in Part III that life develops partly by free will and partly by pre-destination. Our choices dictate the fertility of the environment, affecting the constant rate of acceleration. In other words, we are not in control of the process of life, we are participating in the increase or decrease in the speed of self-ordering of the universe.

For argument's sake, consider what would happen if humanity suddenly decided to stop evolving. If we did not want to participate in the continuing development of life, we could turn off our computers and just stop. I argue that our minds have evolved in a way to make that impossible because we have an innate drive to survive. However, assuming that it was possible, and humanity did stop developing… life would find a way to continue to evolve. Humanity would die out and some other organism would fill the void. Life would continue and some new form of intelligence would emerge.

There might be some confusion in combining the Theory of Continuity with what we know about the fossil record. In the past, evolution appears to have occurred in sudden jumps, not a smooth curve of development. For instance, there are abrupt transitions from sea life to land dwelling animals, and from dinosaurs to mammals. These sudden jumps do not appear to follow a smooth development curve. However, evolution takes on new meaning within the context of the Theory of Continuity. Biological distinctiveness no longer drives evolutionary change, but rather change occurs based on resource constraints on levels of productivity. Biological change is not evolution's only method of increasing productivity. When man discovered fire, it was an increase in productivity with no change in biology. A community of organisms can progress in productivity while remaining unchanged biologically as long as there is spare capacity within the environment. It is only when the current state keeps productivity levels from following the exponential growth curve demanded by the Theory of Continuity that evolution triggers biological change. Biological change is a by-product of the self-organization of the universe. For instance, fish only need to grow lungs to survive on land when oceans become overpopulated. For the fish, land provides an opportunity to access greater resources. Fish develop lungs, and life continues to develop.

We might see evolutionary changes happen again in humans if the environment reached capacity. For instance, if oxygen levels dropped, we would probably see some humans develop with larger lungs, even to the point of creating a new species. This change is necessary to maintain the universe's "quota" for productivity according to the fertility of the environment. This occurs in much the same way in business when a market becomes saturated. Innovators will adapt to create new markets and unlock greater opportunities. The reason humans have not experienced further biological changes is precisely because our intelligence allows us to be so innovative, and as a result, our environment has not yet reached full capacity.

We see this process play out in the modern day as species continue to become extinct. Extinction usually occurs because some other species is using the environment more productively, and takes their place. This is the human story. Humans developed biological technology that differentiated them from apes. Apes lived in the forests, but humans were able to survive equally well on the plains in Africa which gave them access to much larger amounts of resources. Humans' higher level of productivity allowed them to dominate the food chain in environments and gradually settle around the globe. This epic evolutionary story continues today. Developments in R&D drive certain economies to become more or less productive. Power struggles between nations continue as the evolutionary process drives onward. This is also the reason why alien invasion movies are so popular to audiences. It is a representation of our own human history. The fear of an alien attack on humanity is rooted in guilt over the human credit market causing the extinction of other species.

I suggest that each business exists as an extension of the overall process of the evolution of the universe. This understanding frames business decisions in an entirely new way. A business' success depends on survival in an evolutionary environment. In this framework, the concept of "failure" becomes incredibly important.

Failure is what allows growth to happen. Failure is perhaps a poor word choice because society places such a negative connotation on the word. It is really all a matter of perspective. A business initiative might be a failure from a limited viewpoint, but the lessons learned might be the foundation that drives future success in an unexpected area. The more attempts made in a system, failed or successful, will make that system more competitive in an evolutionary environment than a system that makes no attempts. We often do not like to dwell on failure in business. However, mistakes are important. Investors on Wall Street constantly look for winning companies, but that might be the wrong approach. They are better off spending their time looking for companies that experience a big failure, but deal with the mistake in a positive way. Those companies are good investments, at the right stock price (which would probably have just dropped because the company made a mistake). Credit markets that include mechanisms that allow for failure will out-perform over the long term.

I realize some of the ideas in this book may seem controversial. However, they are all based on three simple assumptions.

1. Groups can attain higher production rates than individuals. (The Theory of Inequality)
2. The larger an organization becomes, the harder it is to maintain the same growth rate. (The Pull of Debt)
3. Things will grow faster in a more fertile environment. (The Theory of Credit Markets)

If you believe these three reasonable assumptions to be true, then by extending these assumptions to their logical conclusion suggests the rest of the ideas presented in this book are also valid. It explains why the patterns we find in market dynamics match our observations from biology and physics (The Theory of Continuity).

Currently we tend to think of business, biology, and physics as separate areas of study. Universities are laid out with the different subjects in separate buildings. Physicists study motion, biologists study life, and business people study money. Each area considers their subject unique, requiring its own special set of rules. I challenge people to consider the possibility there is a rule that unites these disciplines. The Theory of Continuity suggests that in all three areas, the laws of the universe govern events by the constraint of the speed of light. Light is everywhere. It is the constant that unites the universe. It is the constraint that molds space-time. It determines the forces of nature. It determines the development of everything we do. It causes life to form and drives the continued growth of everything. All existence is governed by light.

Existential questions

When people ponder their existence, they usually ask two questions:

1. How did we get here?
2. What is the meaning of life?

The previous sections provide a possible scenario to answer the first question. The second question about finding "meaning" is a little more elusive. However, I suggest that credit markets can provide insight into the meaning of life.

This book provides a description of the universe that some may find depressing. Not only am I suggesting that equations dictate our lives, but that humanity is not special. We are merely a blip along the development curve of the universe. One could almost describe the human species as a "side-effect" of ongoing self-organization. We have seen hints of this realization in the history of physics. In 1632, the Inquisition brought Galileo Galilei to trial for his theory that the Earth revolved around the sun. Pope Urban VIII found Galileo's work contradictory to the Bible's teachings that the Earth was the center of the universe. I Chronicles 16:30 (New International Version) states, "Tremble before him, all the

Earth! The world is firmly established; it cannot be moved." The Inquisition used this verse as evidence that the Earth was at the center of the cosmos, and everything else in the universe revolved around us. To avoid torture, Galileo recanted his theories. The Inquisition convicted Galileo of heresy, banned his books, and sentenced him to house arrest for the rest of his life.[55]

This stands as a notable example of how difficult it is for society to accept a theory that says we are not special. Our difficulty stems from our experience that we *feel* there must be some level of meaning. This contradiction in our psychology creates a dilemma. Even though history has proven Galileo right, that the sun, our source of light, is the center of the solar system, and our solar system is but one of many in the universe, we have a hard time accepting the notion of a meaningless existence based on equations.

There is a way to resolve this dilemma. Psychologist Mihaly Csikszentmihalyi defined a concept he called "flow." This is a psychological state when a person feels fully engaged, focused, and experiences enjoyment performing an activity. Flow describes a state of mind often experienced by elite athletes as well as high performers in other fields as diverse as the arts and sciences.[56] People experiencing flow are often engaged in what they consider their "purpose." Purpose is the subject of a large amount of business research, with a wide range of definitions. However, I suggest that the relationship between flow and credit markets provides a very simple and practical definition of purpose.

I propose the definition of purpose is "an individual participating in some activity they generally perform better than others." In the context of credit markets, an individual performing at a high level is contributing to the market's exponential growth curve. If someone does not feel that their activities are positively contributing to their social network, they will feel stress and their role will feel meaningless. These negative feelings are a result of divergence from the course dictated by the Theory of Continuity.

The benefit of this definition is that finding your purpose does not have to be an overwhelming task. It is not necessarily one specific thing. It could be math, athletics, medicine, or even caring for others. Each individual's unique talents and experiences allow them to approach problems differently than anyone else on the planet. This unique perspective, not only makes each one of us special, it is how evolution works. Everyone has the ability to perform some task above average. You do not have to be the best at that task, just better than most. Your unique set of abilities could be the unexpected combination that moves the human race forward.

When people fulfill their purpose, they find meaning in life. Participation in credit markets in a positive way contributes to the ongoing self-organization of the universe. Moreover, fulfilling your purpose feels good. There is a reason why people refer to it as a state of "flow." You are contributing to society in a way that others cannot. You will even find "meaning" in your work. You engage fully with society and the world around you. You are feeling the influence of the speed of light. When you are in a state of flow, you are feeling the hand of God.

Organizational Behavior

Any discussion about credit markets deals with interactions between individuals. As a result, the Theory of Continuity also has implications for a company's organizational behavior. This field of business develops "mental models" to understand employee motivations in the decision process. These models have been extremely useful in understanding workforce behavior, and answering every business leader's biggest question, "How do I get my employees to do what I want?"[57]

In 1964, a scholar named Victor Vroom developed an influential mental model called Expectancy Theory. The theory explains that three factors drive a person's motivation: expectancy, instrumentality, and valence. In a general sense, the model assesses a person's motivation as a function of their ability to see a goal and their ability to reach it. These definitions allow scholars to perform detailed statistical analysis on employee motivation.[58]

Victor Vroom's Expectancy Theory

Expectancy: Effort → Performance (E→P)
Instrumentality: Performance → Outcome (P→O)
Valence: V(R)
Motivational Force (MR) =
Expectancy x Instrumentality x Valence

Most models follow a similar approach where an employer can achieve a desired outcome by intervening at different points along some decision making process. These models suggest that if you provide an individual with rewards, they will perform a task with the appropriate level of motivation. However, the Theory of Continuity suggests a significantly different approach. Since the laws of nature partially drive outcomes, it is possible for an organization to reach a desired outcome without *any* intervention by the employer or the decision maker. Individuals will develop themselves based on the fertility of the environment. This may seem like a radical notion, but it is simply a restatement of the story of human existence. As a species, we exist in a certain environment, and over the millennium, we have developed on our own.

The Theory of Continuity suggests two approaches: the business leader's perspective and the individual's perspective (or high and low productivity). Both parties want to maximize their effectiveness. As discussed earlier, the fertility of the environment (*F*) is the only variable we can influence to increase future cash flows. This suggests that for business leaders to increase production levels, they need to increase the fertility of the system rather than change individuals' decisions. From the employee perspective, each person should strive to reach a state of flow, which will outperform others within the same social network.

Organizational Behavior under the Theory of Continuity

- Place an individual in an adequately fertile environment and they will develop themselves.
- Individuals in areas of high productivity gain the greatest effectiveness by improving the fertility of the environment.
- Individuals in areas of low productivity gain the greatest effectiveness by achieving a state of flow.

The main difference between the Theory of Continuity and a mental model like Victor Vroom's, is the Theory of Continuity is describing relationships on a larger scale. The Theory of Continuity says nothing about the outcome of a single decision. Whether the decision is positive or negative does not matter. The Theory of Continuity explains that the combination of all the many decisions, positive and negative, over an extended period, will result in a certain level of productivity.

Putting this framework into practice can significantly improve performance. Imagine a company where all the employees view their jobs as fulfilling a "purpose" instead of "work." This would be a significant contrast from most other businesses where people usually use the term "work" with negative connotations. People do not like work. People consider work a chore, and people look forward to vacation from work. If instead, people are fulfilling a "purpose," then they are not merely performing a task. Employees with purpose contribute to something they are good at and enjoy. They participate in the process of growth. I suggest that a business with such a workforce would not only be vastly more productive, it would create a sustainable competitive advantage.

As an example, consider your own employment. What if instead of doing work, you were doing things that inspired you? Imagine coming to your job every day and spending the whole day being inspired. We all have moments of inspiration occasionally, but when we are fulfilling our purpose, our jobs become an inspirational experience. Now consider a list of tasks you work on during an average day. What if you did more of the things you find inspiring, and stopped doing the things you hated? The items on your list that you find inspiring are probably the areas you are contributing the most to the credit market of your business. If you find nothing about your job inspiring, you are probably in the wrong job. This approach to business makes the role of a manager a life altering position. A manager is connecting people with the areas where they can find inspiration.

A practical example of applying these ideas would be a business leader's approach to handling what we commonly refer to as the "office jerk." This is a personality type we have all encountered. It is someone who is insensitive, mean-spirited, and generally a bully. Most businesses usually tolerate these characteristics if the individual is contributing to company profits. This management approach is captured in the popular saying "It's not personal, it's business." However, the Theory of Continuity suggests that business is personal, because productivity is a function of the network of social relationships. One insensitive person can create a hostile environment that seriously compromises a company's ability to grow. In an evolutionary environment, you are only as strong as your team. It is more important to create a fertile environment that encourages employees to take calculated risks. The long-term success of the organization relies on the ability of everyone in the social network to innovate.

Business Strategy

Traditional strategy methods used in business are similar to moving pieces around a chessboard. Each player is in control of a certain number of pieces on a defined playing field and the goal is to out-maneuver the opponent. For example, Jay B. Barney, one of the foremost scholars on business strategy, opens his book Gaining and Sustaining Competitive Advantage with examples of strategies to win at blackjack.[59] However, as previously explained, the analogy of blackjack does not fully capture the added influence of physical laws after the hand is dealt. The Theory of Continuity, however, suggests a different approach to business strategy: We are not completely in control of the rules of the game. We only influence one variable related to growth, because the laws of nature determine the rest of the equation.

A more accurate example of business strategy is making moves on a chessboard that grows and evolves on its own. The winning player is the person who can take advantage of opportunities within the dynamic environment. What follows is a list of practical strategies aligned with the Theory of Continuity. This is not a comprehensive list, but rather a starting place to think differently about business strategy.

Find fertile ground. This is a strategy commonly referred to as "location, location, location." Choosing the right location has historically been an essential element for business success. The Theory of Continuity explains the relationship between location and growth through the variable of fertility of the environment. The better the location is, the greater the return on assets.

We can see the impact of location in several examples. A barrel of oil would generate higher productivity in a first world country than a third world country. We see this in varying productivity data from different countries. Other examples highlight the idea that physical location has become less important. Instead, location can be determined through positioning in the market. Apple created a differentiated brand in the smart phone market, and this "location" contributed to significant company growth. Companies can now also improve the fertility of their locations in a number of ways ranging from the use of technology to improving company culture. Google is an example of a company that used technology to create a successful online location and created a culture that regularly produces innovations.

Create diversity. Diversity is something rarely mentioned in company strategic plans. However, the Theory of Continuity suggests that diversity is an important driver of growth. The mix of ideas provided by a diversity of backgrounds creates the palette of options from which evolution selects: the greater the number of options, the more fertile the environment. An organization with limited diversity has a limited palette of evolutionary options. Therefore, a diverse organization has a greater potential to discover new ways to grow and out-compete the market in the long-term.

Celebrate failure. Failure is another subject that companies are not likely to mention in strategic plans. However, failure is one of the most important aspects in a healthy evolutionary system. Evolution works because you generate multiple failures to discover the greatest success. Business often works in the opposite way. If an employee makes a mistake, management often quickly punishes them. The intention is to motivate the employee to stop making mistakes. However, the message the employee receives is to stop taking risks. Companies should view failure as opportunities to see how employees are innovating and what options create the most success. Failure is part of the engine of evolution. Encouraging failure is one way to fuel that engine and create a more fertile environment for growth.

Align with highly productive entities. Credit arrangements make both parties better off. If you can find entities that are more productive than you and form credit arrangements, your position will benefit. Individuals want to work for businesses. Businesses want to contract with larger organizations. Each step of the chain is an opportunity to create value through transferring assets to an area of higher productivity. Managers can also apply this concept to individual parts of the business. This is why outsourcing creates value for companies. Outsourcing is a strategic analysis of what areas of the company are sources of high productivity, and what areas can perform better outside the company.

Partake in as much technology transfer as possible. Creating a credit arrangement with a more productive company is only the first step in outsourcing. The second step is to figure out how the other company has higher productivity than you do, and transfer that knowledge back to your company. Any relationship has the possibility to learn something new. Bringing in best practices to increase a business' own productivity can generate wealth.

Food production is a good example of this strategy. It often makes sense to outsource food production rather than have individuals grow their own food. However, this creates a risk if the social network fails to retain knowledge about farming or learn about new farming technology. For example, if a country imports the majority of food production without some knowledge management of the process, they create a risk. The supplier is in a position to control their relationship. This might seem like an extreme example, but we frequently experience the same thing as individuals. We might outsource our medical or legal problems to experts. Without some form of knowledge management, others could take advantage of the relationship. In other words, this strategy restates the familiar phrase "knowledge is power."

Integrate into the economic system as much as possible. Many examples show that participating in economic markets provides more benefits than working alone. The Theory of Continuity supports this idea, because the more people that create credit arrangements, the better off society will be overall. The world economy is a massive system. Successful businesses find ways to become an important part of that system. When people integrate a product into their lives, they are making a credit arrangement for that activity. An integrated product creates high demand and generates future cash flows. It is in a business' best interest to make as many credit arrangements as possible, or in other words, to become fully integrated with their social network.

Productivity is power. In any business setting there are many different types of power (legitimate, physical, etc.). Productivity is the source of power that drives the "invisible hand" of economic activity. We often think of banks as powerful, but in an economic sense, they have low productivity and therefore low power. Banks rely on outside entities to be productive and make them money through debt payments. This translates into social dynamics. In a team of people, the person with the highest productivity has the most power in an economic sense, regardless of the person's title. It is easy in business to fixate on dollar values. This can often be misleading without understanding the underlying productivity levels. For instance, a business can hit a target for a certain cash value in their bank accounts, but fail to improve productivity. When businesses target strategic goals on productivity, the business is likely to drive growth and out-compete in the market.

The Theory of Continuity requires a fundamental shift in how we think about business strategy. This new strategy works through cooperation and inspiration rather than selfishness and exploitation. It provides a new answer to the ultimate strategic question "how do I win?" The organizations that out-perform over the long-term are those that create fertile environments that provide for future growth.

Business Strategy under the Theory of Continuity

Organizations that out-perform over the long-term are those that create fertile environments that provide for future growth.

The winning player is the one who can take advantage of opportunities within the dynamic environment.

- Find fertile ground
- Create diversity
- Celebrate failure
- Align with highly productive entities
- Partake in as much technology transfer as possible
- Integrate into the economic system as much as possible
- Productivity is power

As is the case with most strategy discussions, it is easy to make recommendations, but it is much more difficult to implement them. Each of the seven strategies suggested above are very difficult to embrace. They require building a unique systems approach to business. However, if implemented, this difficulty becomes a strength. Other companies will also find the strategies difficult to emulate, creating a sustainable competitive advantage.

True Love

In a completely honest discussion of business, it is necessary to discuss the one topic that is truly motivating everyone... true love. I have spent the majority of this book discussing money, power, and sex. However, when you strip that all away, all anyone ever really wants is love. It is the real motivator behind all our actions. The pursuit of money and power is really just a means to take care of the people you find meaningful in your life. It is true that sex is a strong, powerful biological driver, but that is not what we talk about as a society when it comes to relationships. We talk about love.

What is love? Philosophers have debated this simple question since the beginning of civilization. We tell stories about the great romances in history. We do completely irrational things in the name of love, and afterwards feel that it is all worth it. After much discussion for thousands of years, we are still both confused and captivated by the subject.

While I do not presume to know the answer, we can find some intriguing insights through credit markets. People feel love when they are wanted, needed, or reciprocating those feelings for someone else. Love does not have the same formalized debits and credits of debt arrangements, but it does occur through the same interconnected network of people. Individuals create value for their community and form relationships with others who do the same for them. As a group, we "complete" each other. In this way, love is a positive impact on a network of people.

To be without love is terrifying. One of the favorite stories retold through history is of the shipwrecked sailor on a deserted island. It is curious that life in a tropical paradise should be so terrifying. It captures our imagination because love is an essential part of the human equation. When we are alone, we cannot participate in credit markets, and we cannot experience love.

I propose that love is the emotional response humans have evolved to encourage growth. Love motivates us to be part of the magic of relationships. Love motivates us to become better people. It is the source of our most memorable moments. We want to be part of a marriage, a family, or a friendship that is meaningful. Love is the true driver behind business.

This is the message behind the Theory of Continuity. It creates the link between profits and love. The equations in this book explain how the relationships in our social networks drive productivity. It is not just about business success; it is about success in life.

The Theory of Continuity even goes beyond love. We connect, not only, to our social networks, we connect to the universe itself. All that we are and everything we do connects through the fabric of space-time. Just like gravity is constrained by the speed of light, so too are our processes. Our interactions follow natural laws, as they play a part in the self-organization of the universe. The next time you take a walk, look at the people, trees, and insects around you. It is all business, governing each action. With this new framework, humanity has the chance to participate in this ongoing development. The Theory of Continuity provides an exciting opportunity for the diverse fields of business, biology, and physics to work together to better understand our role in the universe.

APPENDIX 1: CREATING A COMPUTER SIMULATION

Computer simulations create a theoretical universe to test economic theories. A simulation usually consists of a set of assumptions, a list of constraints, a number of mathematical equations, and a series of instructions. If you want to know something, simulations provide a way to test it. Simulations are a way to determine outcomes of different economic situations under specific conditions. In a business, it is a useful tool to forecast different strategies. The goal is to use financial equations that mirror economic reality. If a financial model can replicate economic activity in real life, it is likely to predict cash flows accurately. This allows users to make better business decisions.

Computer simulations can become extremely complex. This section will provide a very simple example. Part I discusses an example of two individuals entering into a debt arrangement. This example uses the following assumptions (**Figure 68**).

ASSUMPTIONS (per period)

	Output	Cost	FTE	Starting Assets	Cost of Capital
X	5	2	1	5	.08
Y	1	2	1	5	.08

Figure 68. Simulation assumptions

Output is some unit of value/time created by the knowledge, equipment, and talent of the entity.
Cost is the number of units used to create the output each period.
Production = Output - Cost
FTE (Full-time equivalent) is the unit of labor. If an individual only worked half time (.5 FTEs), then they would only produce half the output.
1 Unit = $1

These assumptions allow us to evaluate the performance of this social unit over a defined period. The simulation will use the following equations (**Figure 69, Figure 70**). These equations describe that the total production for x every period is 3 while the production for y is -1. The costs for y are greater than the output resulting in negative production. This approach produces the timeline below (**Figure 71**).

$$P_x = (O_x - C_x) * FTE_x$$
$$P = Production\ per\ FTE;\ O = Output\ per\ FTE;$$
$$C = Cost\ per\ FTE;$$
$$FTE = Number\ of\ Fulltime\ equivalents$$

Figure 69. Equation for individual production per period.

$$P_S = \sum_{i=1}^{S} P_i$$

Figure 70. Equation for production of society per period.

TIMELINE

	0	1	2	3	4	5
X	$5.00	$8.00	$11.00	$14.00	$17.00	$20.00
Y	$5.00	$4.00	$3.00	$2.00	$1.00	$0.00
Total	$10.00	$12.00	$14.00	$16.00	$18.00	$20.00

Figure 71. Scenario 1 timeline.

To create a second scenario, period zero becomes a decision point with the following rules (**Figure 72**). These rules describe that an individual will self-identify as having high productivity, if the expected production level exceeds the potential value of debt payments from their assets. This determines whether someone will choose to use their own assets to produce, or give their assets to someone with higher productivity to use. In this case, *x* self-identifies as high productivity and *y* self-identifies as low productivity. The group enters into a debt arrangement in period zero that extends for the next five periods. *X* uses assets from both individuals to create higher production for the group as shown in the timeline below (**Figure 73**). Group production increases from four units per period in Scenario 1 to six units per period in Scenario 2.

$1)\ i = High\ productivity; if\ P_i > |D_i|$
$2)\ i = Low\ productivity; if\ |D_i| > P_i$
$3)\ if\ self\ selection\ occurs, assets\ transfer$
$and\ principal\ is\ repaid\ in\ equal$
$payments\ over\ five\ periods$
$with\ 8\%\ interest$
$4)\ the\ value\ of\ one\ FTE\ is\ 1\ unit\ per\ period$
$5)\ the\ PV\ for\ five\ periods\ of\ \$1\ payments$
$is\ \$3.99$

Figure 72. Scenario rules.

ASSUMPTIONS

	Capacity	Cost	FTE	Starting Wealth	Cost of Capital
X	5	2	2	6	.08
Y	1	2	0	0	.08

TIMELINE

	0	1	2	3	4	5
X	$8.99	$13.99	$18.99	$23.99	$28.99	$33.99
Y	$1.01	$2.01	$3.01	$4.01	$5.01	$6.01
Total	$10.00	$16.00	$22.00	$28.00	$34.00	$40.00

Figure 73. Scenario 2 timeline.

Note that x uses the additional assets to purchase an FTE. Y then produces at the production level of x. Even though y does not utilize its own output, it is still increasing in wealth over five periods.

This model is different from the approach normally used in a financial simulation for this transaction. Financial equations normally describe a transaction from one party's perspective. This means the only assets counted would be the specific debt instrument, ignoring the extra production created. X only accounts for receiving the funds in period zero and then returning those funds in the subsequent periods with interest. Likewise, y only accounts for its side of the transaction. The result is the timeline below (**Figure 74**) where total production for the society remains the same. This approach misses the social dynamics of the transaction. Comparing this description with scenario 1 illustrates the discrepancy between the two methods. In scenario 3, the forecast for x is *worse* than if x had produced alone. Under this outcome, there is no incentive to form a debt arrangement. Of course, in a real market situation, there is an incentive to form debt arrangements, which illustrates why Scenario 2 is a preferable simulation.

TIMELINE

	0	1	2	3	4	5
X	$8.99	$10.99	$12.99	$14.99	$16.99	$18.99
Y	$1.01	$1.01	$1.01	$1.01	$1.01	$1.01
Total	$10.00	$12.00	$14.00	$16.00	$18.00	$20.00

Figure 74. Scenario 3 timeline.

APPENDIX 2: A REVIEW OF SPECIAL RELATIVITY

This appendix provides a brief summary of Special Relativity. You can find all of the following information in any entry-level college physics book.[60]

The speed of light is one of the few constants in the universe. No matter the situation, light always travels at the same speed (**Figure 75**). This constant has held true in many different experiments.

$$Speed\ of\ light = 299{,}792{,}458\ m/s$$

Figure 75. Constant for the speed of light.

The example of a moving car illustrates the significance of this constant. Imagine a person sits on the side of a road. A car drives past and the driver of the car throws a ball out the window ahead of the moving car. The ball is traveling at a faster speed from the perspective of the person on the side of the road, than from the perspective of the person in the car. The motion of the ball is relative to the observer (**Figure 76**). However, the speed of light is not relative; it is constant. If the car in motion turned on its headlights, both individuals would experience the light moving away from the car at the speed of light (**Figure 76**). The difference occurs because the ball has mass and the light does not.

$$\textbf{\textit{Person on the side of the road}}:$$
$$Speed\ of\ the\ ball = Speed\ of\ the\ car + speed\ of\ the\ thrown\ object$$
$$Speed\ of\ the\ light\ from\ the\ headlights = Speed\ of\ light$$

$$\textbf{\textit{Person in the car}}:$$
$$Speed\ of\ the\ ball = Speed\ of\ the\ thrown\ object$$
$$Speed\ of\ the\ light\ from\ the\ headlights = Speed\ of\ light$$

Figure 76. Equations for objects in motion relative to observers.

Einstein explained this seeming contradiction with the Theory of Special Relativity. The theory explains that since a light beam cannot change its speed, space and time must warp to accommodate it. This seems contrary to our experience, in which space and time seem to be constant. However, Einstein's equations explain that the faster an object travels, time will slow down and space will contract in the direction of the motion. One evidence of this is the motion of satellites around the Earth in the Global Positioning System (GPS). The clocks on the satellites run slower than the clocks on the surface of the Earth by seven microseconds per day, exactly the amount predicted by the equations in Einstein's Theory of Special Relativity.

Since the speed of light is a constant, it acts as a cosmic speed limit. Objects with mass can never reach the speed of light. Einstein expressed this concept in his famous equation (**Figure 77**).

$$E = mc^2$$
$$E = energy; m = mass;$$
$$c = constant\ for\ the\ speed\ of\ light$$

Figure 77. Einstein's equation of Special Relativity (simplified version).

What is commonly misunderstood is that this is not the full equation. Einstein proposed that the relationship between mass and energy describes a right triangle (**Figure 78**). Based on the Pythagorean Theorem, the full equation is as follows (**Figure 79**).

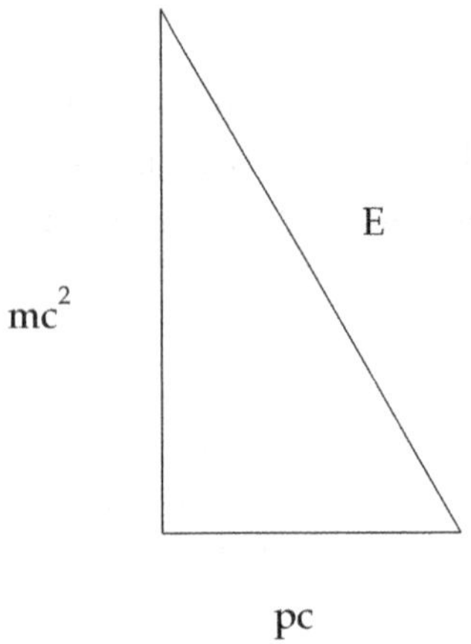

Figure 78. The relationship between mass and energy described by a right triangle.

$$E^2 = (pc)^2 + (mc^2)^2$$
$$E = energy; m = mass; p = momentum;$$
$$c = constant\ for\ the\ speed\ of\ light$$

Figure 79. Einstein's equation of Special Relativity (full version)

This triangle illustrates how changes in mass and speed relate to energy because the speed of light is constant. This triangle relationship was Einstein's great insight. His famous equation merely describes the effect of this relationship. Einstein's triangle explains the following effects.

1. In situations common to human experience, speed occurs on a scale much smaller than the speed of light. In these cases, the side of the triangle representing momentum is very short. This explains why humans do not experience the difference in energy as determined through Einstein's equations versus Newton's classical laws of physics.
2. In more extreme cases where the speed of an object approaches the speed of light, we see this side of the triangle become very long. Because the longest side of the triangle represents energy, it will always be longer than the side describing the object's momentum. Therefore, the speed of an object will never reach the speed of light, because the energy will still have to be greater. There would not be enough energy in the universe to move an object at the speed of light unless the object's mass were zero, changing the triangle to a straight line relationship between speed and energy. This is why the speed of light is the speed limit for the universe.

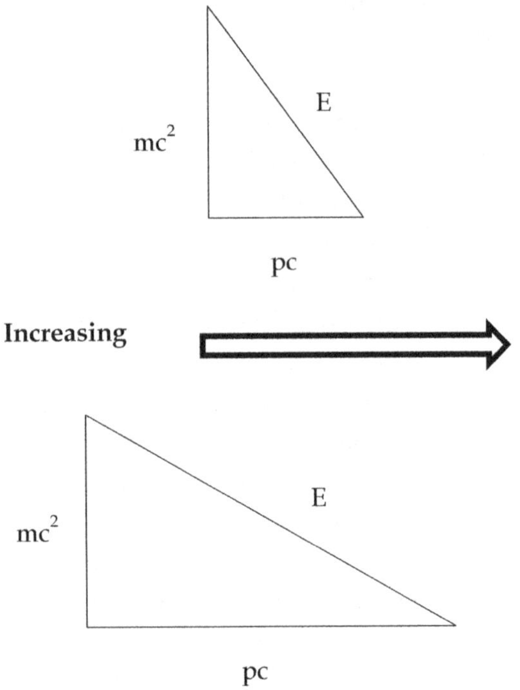

Figure 80. Triangle expands as velocity increases.

3. The relationship between mass and energy also explains why the speed of light is a constant. The equation is not just describing the speed of "light," but the speed of any particle with zero mass that exists as pure energy (**Figure 81**). Such a particle has to travel at the speed *c*.

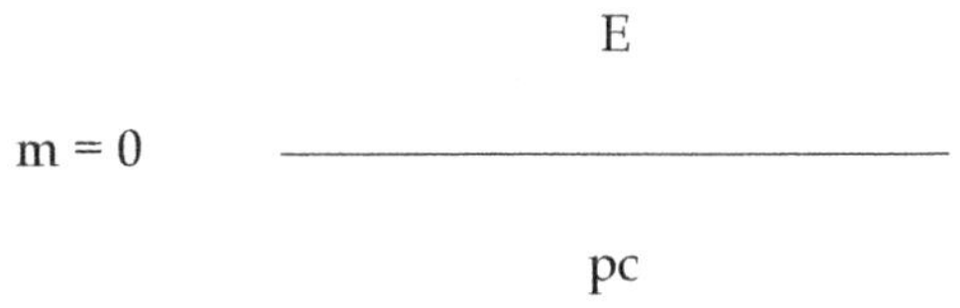

Figure 81. Triangle when mass equals zero.

4. In the same way, if speed were zero, an object's mass would have a direct relationship with energy. The triangle shows that when an object is at rest (p=0) the energy side of the triangle is the same length as the mass side of the triangle (**Figure 82**). In other words, $E=mc^2$. An object at rest has a certain amount of pure energy related to the speed of light.

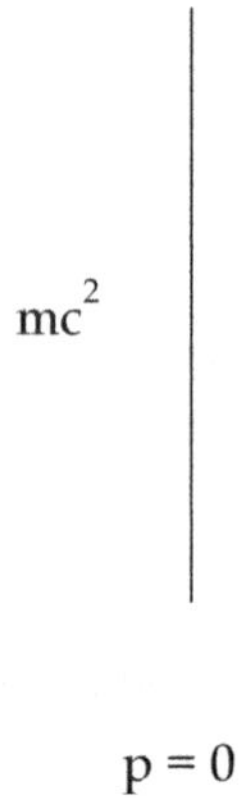

Figure 82. Triangle when velocity equals zero.

5. The energy side of the triangle splits into two parts: Kinetic and "rest-energy." Kinetic energy is involved in the motion of the object and "rest-energy" is the energy of the object itself. If the object is at zero speed, the entire length of the energy side is equal to an object's "rest-energy." Each increase in the object's speed requires an increase in energy above the object's "rest-energy," or the part of the energy side that represents kinetic energy. That is why the faster an object moves, the more energy it takes. In other words, it becomes heavier. Likewise, the

more mass an object has, the more energy it takes to move.

6. All energy is "conserved," meaning energy is not created or destroyed, it just changes to other forms. Therefore Einstein's equation, $E=mc^2$, explains how mass can be translated into energy and back again into mass. That is how Einstein's equation led to the creation of the atomic bomb, where the mass of an extremely small object (like an atom) can release an enormous amount of energy.

Two astronomers, Andrew Crommelin and Arthur Eddinton, conducted the first major experiment that supported Einstein's Theory of Special Relativity. On May 29, 1919, a solar eclipse gave the astronomers a chance to evaluate the light from stars where the light beams were traveling close to the sun. Crommelin observed from Sobral, Brazil, and Eddinton observed on the island of Principe off the coast of Africa. The astronomers took photos of the positions of stars before and during the eclipse. They confirmed that space around the sun was "bending" according to Einstein's calculations. The Theory of Special Relativity predicts that a ray of light traveling close to the sun will appear to bend by 1.75 arcseconds (or a right triangle that is 1 inch high and 1.9 miles long).

TABLE OF FIGURES

INDEX

END NOTES

Introduction

[1] Miller, Rich, Joshua Zumbrun and Niklas Magnusson. "Fama, Shiller, Hansen Win Nobel Prize for Asset-Price Work." Oct 14, 2013. Bloomberg.
Available online at:
<http://www.bloomberg.com/news/2013-10-14/fama-hansen-shiller-share-nobel-economics-prize-academy-says.html>

[2] The Eight Fundamental Finance Equations with descriptions and methodology can be found in any Finance text. Bode, Zvi, Alex Kane, and Alan J. Marcus. Investments. McGraw-Hill Irwin: New York. 2009.

Part I: The Theory of Inequality

[3] Kieso, Donald E., Jerry J. Weygandt, and Terry D. Warfield. Intermediate Accounting. 14th Edition. John Wiley & Sons, Inc.: New Jersey. 2012.

[4] Milanovic, Branko. "Global Income Inequality by the Numbers: in History and Now." The World Bank. [White Paper] November 2012.

[5] Beveridge, Thomas. A Primer on Microeconomics. Business Expert Press: New York. 2013. Chp 6 "Perfect Competition in the Long Run"

[6] Dobeck, Mark F. and Euel Elliott. Money. Greenwood Press: Connecticut. 2007. Chp 1 "The History and Evolution of Money: A Look Back."

[7] Graeber, David. Debt: The First 5,000 Years. First Melville House Printing: Brooklyn, New York. May 2011. Chp 2 "The Myth of Barter"

[8] Melissa Hogenboom. "Howling wolves gives clue to top dog" 22 Aug 2013. BBC News.
Available online at: <http://www.bbc.co.uk/news/science-environment-23767354>

Francesco Mazzini, Simon W. Townsend, Zsófia Virányi, Friederike Range. "Wolf Howling Is Mediated by Relationship Quality Rather Than Underlying Emotional Stress." Current Biology, Available online 22 August 2013.
Available online at:
<http://www.sciencedirect.com/science/article/pii/S0960982213008233>

[9] Financial Crisis Inquiry Commission. United States. The Financial Crisis Inquiry Report. 2011.

[10] Barney, Jay B. Gaining and Sustaining Competitive Advantage. Third Edition. Pearson: New Jersey. 2007. Pg.

Part II: The Pull of Debt

[11] U.S. Department of Commerce: Bureau of Economic Analysis. Current-Dollar Gross Domestic Product. Accessed Sept 2013. <http://www.bea.gov/national/index.htm#gdp>

[12] Young, Hugh D., Roger A. Freedman. University Physics. 13th Edition. Pearson Education: San Francisco. 2012. Pg. 52

[13] U.S. Department of Commerce: Bureau of Economic Analysis. Current-Dollar Gross Domestic Product. Accessed Sept 2013. <http://www.bea.gov/national/index.htm#gdp>

[14] Hull, John C. Options, Futures, and other Derivatives: Seventh Edition. Pearson Prentice Hall: New Jersey. 2008. Pg. 277

[15] Graeber, David. Debt: The First 5,000 Years. First Melville House Printing: Brooklyn, New York. May 2011. Chp 1 "On the Experience of Moral Confusion"

[16] Ibid. Chp 5 "A Brief Treatise on the Moral Grounds of Economic Relations"

[17] Ibid. Chp 5 "A Brief Treatise on the Moral Grounds of Economic Relations"

[18] Livio, Mario. The Golden Ratio: The Story of Phi, the World's Most Astonishing Number. Broadway Books: New York. 2002. Chp 5 "Son of Good Nature"

[19] Ibid. Chp 5 "Son of Good Nature"

[20] Ibid. Chp 1 "Prelude to a Number"

[21] Ibid. Chp 1 "Prelude to a Number"

[22] Ibid. Chp 5 "Son of Good Nature"

[23] Rutishauser, Rolf. "Symmetry in plants." *Series in Mathematical Biology and Medicine, vol 4*, World Scientific Publishing : River Edge, NJ. 1998. Pg. 203.
Available online at:
<http://books.google.com/books?id=XpVG1UwncogC&printsec=frontcover&source=gbs_ge_summary_r&cad=0#v=onepage&q&f=false>

[24] S.L. Basin. "The Fibonacci Sequence As It Appears In Nature" Fibonacci Quarterly, vol 1 (1963), pages 53-57. Available online at: <http://www.fq.math.ca/Scanned/1-1/basin.pdf>

[25] Kuczmarski RJ, Ogden CL, Guo SS, et al. "2000 CDC Growth Charts for the United States: Methods and Development." [White Paper] *Vital and Health Statistics, Series 11, Number 246.* Department for Health and Human Services (Center for Disease Control and Prevention, National Center for Health Statistics) : Hyattsville, MD. May 2002. Pg143

[26] Livio, Mario. The Golden Ratio: The Story of Phi, the World's Most Astonishing Number. Broadway Books: New York. 2002. Chp 6

[27] Graeber, David. Debt: The First 5,000 Years. First Melville House Printing: Brooklyn, New York. May 2011. Chp 5 "A Brief Treatise on the Moral Grounds of Economic Relations"

Part III: The Theory of Credit Markets

[28] Bode, Zvi, Alex Kane, and Alan J. Marcus. Investments. McGraw-Hill Irwin: New York. 2009. Pg 345

[29] Ibid. Pg 103

[30] Malkiel, Burton G. A Random Walk Down Wall Street. W.W. Norton & Company: New York. 2012. Chp 1 "Firm Foundations and Castles in the Air"

[31] Koller, Tim, Marc Goedhart, and David Wessels. McKinsey & Company. Valuation: Measuring and Managing the Value of Companies. Fourth Edition. John Wiley & Sons : Hoboken, NJ. 2005. Pg 7

Part IV: Practical Applications

[32] Bode, Zvi, Alex Kane, and Alan J. Marcus. Investments. McGraw-Hill Irwin: New York. 2009. Pg 592

[33] Koller, Tim, Marc Goedhart, and David Wessels: McKinsey & Company. Valuation: Measuring and Managing the Value of Companies. Fourth Edition. John Wiley & Sons: Hoboken, NJ. 2005. Pg. 275

[34] Ibid. Pg. 279

[35] Ibid. Pg. 275

[36] Ibid. Pg. 277

Part V: The Theory of Continuity

[37] Young, Hugh D., Roger A. Freedman. University Physics. 13th Edition. Pearson Education: San Francisco. 2012. Pg. 49

[38] Ibid. Pg. 1248

[39] Ibid. Pg. 403

[40] Ibid. Pg. 1250

[41] Ibid. Pg. 1250

[42] Ibid. Pg. 1250

[43] Ibid. Pg. 1328

[44] Weatherall, James Owen. The Physics of Wall Street. Houghton Mifflin Harcourt: New York. 2013. Chp 2 "Swimming Upstream"

[45] Ibid. Chp 1 "Primordial Seeds"

[46] Ibid. Chp 1 "Primordial Seeds"

[47] The World Bank. GDP in current US$. <http://data.worldbank.org/indicator/NY.GDP.MKTP.CD/countries/1W?display=default>

[48] The World Bank. GDP in current US$. <http://data.worldbank.org/indicator/NY.GDP.MKTP.CD/countries/1W?display=default>

[49] Williams, Tony. The Jamestown Experiment: The Remarkable Story of the Enterprising Colony and the Unexpected Results that Shaped America. Sourcebooks: Naperville, IL. 2011. Pg 56

[50] Ibid. Pg 20

[51] Ibid. Pg 33

[52] Ibid. Pg 194

[53] Young, Hugh D., Roger A. Freedman. University Physics. 13th Edition. Pearson Education: San Francisco. 2012. Pg. 176

[54] McKay, Chris. "What is Life?--and How Do We Search for It on Other Worlds?" PLoS Biology 2(9): e302. Sep. 14, 2004. Available online at: <http://www.plosbiology.org/article/info:doi/10.1371/journal.pbio.0020302>

[55] Shlain, Leonard. Art & Physics: Parallel Visions in Space, Time, and Light. HarperCollins: New York. 1991. Pg 62

[56] Csikszentmihalyi, Mihaly. Flow: The Psychology of Optimal Experience. HarperCollins: New York. 2009. Chapter 2: "The Anatomy of Consciousness"

[57] Hellriegel, Don and John W. Slocum Jr. Organizational Behavior. 12th Edition. South-western Cengage Learning: Mason, OH. 2009. Pg 4

[58] George, Jennifer M. and Gareth R. Jones. Understanding and Managing Organizational Behavior. 3rd Edition. Prentice Hall: Upper Saddle River, NJ. 2002. Pg. 197

[59] Barney, Jay B. Gaining and Sustaining Competitive Advantage: Third Edition. Pearson Prentice Hall: Upper Saddle River, NJ. 2007. Pg. 1

Appendix 2: A Review of Special Relativity

[60] Young, Hugh D., Roger A. Freedman. University Physics. 13th Edition. Pearson Education: San Francisco. 2012. Pg. 1223

Made in the USA
Coppell, TX
07 February 2026

71413818R00128